HOW-TO cookbook for KIDS

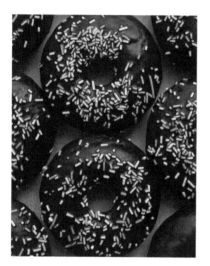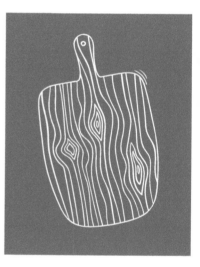

HOW-TO
cookbook
FOR KIDS

50 EASY RECIPES
TO LEARN THE BASICS

Nancy Polanco

ROCKRIDGE
PRESS

For general information on our other products and services or to obtain technical support, please contact our Customer Care Department within the United States at (866) 744-2665, or outside the United States at (510) 253-0500.

Rockridge Press publishes its books in a variety of electronic and print formats. Some content that appears in print may not be available in electronic books, and vice versa.

TRADEMARKS: Rockridge Press and the Rockridge Press logo are trademarks or registered trademarks of Callisto Media Inc. and/or its affiliates, in the United States and other countries, and may not be used without written permission. All other trademarks are the property of their respective owners. Rockridge Press is not associated with any product or vendor mentioned in this book.

Interior and Cover Designer: Linda Snorina
Art Producer: Samantha Ulban
Editor: Justin Hartung
Production Editor: Emily Sheehan
Production Manager: Holly Haydash

Photography © 2021 Annie Martin, cover and pp. ii, iix, 4, 9, 10, 22, 26, 40, 44, 56, 62, 72, 87, 90, 96, 108; © Evi Abeler, pp. 14, 15, 16, 17, 18, 20; © Jennifer Chong, pp. 18, 19, 20. Food Styling by Julian Mancuso. Illustrations used under license Shutterstock.

Cover image: One-Pot Cheddar and Sausage Rigatoni, page 80

Paperback ISBN: 978-1-64876-322-9
eBook ISBN: 978-1-64876-323-6
R0

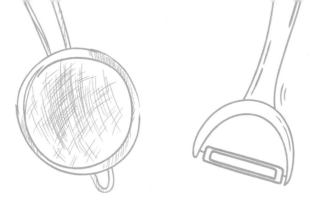

For my beloved parents,
Francisco and Milagro,
and my angels
Gabriella, Michaela, and Darasak.
Thank you for always believing in me.

Contents

Introduction

Cooking can fill you with a sense of pride. The more you do it, the more you'll enjoy making tasty, satisfying food. I hope this book will help you pursue your cooking dreams, whether it's surprising your family with breakfast or being able to cook exactly what you're craving.

Growing up, my mother, Milagro, made us delicious meals in her humble kitchen. She didn't cook super fancy food, just comforting rustic meals with simple ingredients. She taught me that a dish doesn't need to be complicated to be good—it just needs to taste great.

Watching my mom at the stove is what made me fall in love with cooking. I became a better cook by experimenting with new recipes and being open to different flavors. Now I can be inventive in the kitchen and create dishes that my kids and my blog readers love. I share this passion for cooking with my husband, Darasak. My daughters, Gabby and Michaela, love being in the kitchen, too. They enjoy trying new recipes, and it's a joy to see them do their best and grow as cooks.

I'm so excited for you to learn new kitchen skills that will help you cook what you like and grow as a chef. The recipes will get more challenging in each chapter, so it's best to start with the basic recipes first. Happy cooking—you got this!

CHAPTER 1

HOW TO GET READY

I'm sure you can't wait to get started with your first recipe. But before we start chopping and stirring, let's walk through some important cooking rules. Understanding the basics can make the whole cooking process a lot easier and even take a meal to the next level! In this chapter, we'll learn about the tools and ingredients you'll always want to have on hand. We'll also cover safety and preparation tips that will help you get comfortable in the kitchen and ready to cook. Let's get started!

Thin-Crust Pepperoni Pizza PAGE 74

SAFETY FIRST!

Cooking can be so much fun, but there are important safety rules to know before doing anything in the kitchen.

Sharp Things

- If you're just learning how to use a knife, make sure there's an adult around who can watch you and answer any questions.
- A dull knife is unsafe, so keep yours sharpened. Ask an adult to show you how a knife sharpener works.
- Never run with a knife. Keep the tip of the blade pointed down when walking with a knife, and always pass the knife with the handle pointed toward the person you are handing it to.
- Place knives away from the edge of the counter if you need to step away, and never try to catch a falling knife.
- When using a knife, position your other hand away from the blade and watch as you cut your food. The fingers of your other hand should **never** be under or close to the blade of the knife.
- Curl the fingers of the hand that's not holding the knife into a "C" and place your curved fingers on top of the food to hold it in place. Tuck your thumb inward. This protects your fingertips.
- Ask an adult before using a blender, which has very sharp blades, and have an adult with you while you're using one. **Never** stick your hand in a blender. Make sure your hands are dry before plugging the blender in, and always secure the lid before turning it on. Never place a utensil in the blender while it's on; if you want to stir ingredients, turn the blender off first.

Hot Things

- Always let an adult know that you are going to use the stove or oven, and ask for help if you need to. Keep anything that can catch fire (like kitchen towels or oven mitts) away from stove burners. Never leave the kitchen when you're cooking.

- Before you turn on the oven, make sure there's nothing inside. Be sure to always wear oven mitts when handling anything coming out of the oven as well as when panfrying, removing lids from pots, and doing other work at the stove. After cooking, make sure all appliances, the stovetop, and the oven are turned off.
- Keep a watchful eye on the stove, and if any food drops near the burners, to avoid burning yourself, do not try to pick it up. If there's a pan fire, don't throw water on it. Call an adult, and they can use baking soda or a lid to smother the flame instead.
- Never pour water into hot oil—it can vaporize quickly and cause a fire. Water on the ingredients in the pan can also cause hot oil to splash you. Before cooking, try to remove as much moisture as you can from the ingredients; pat them down with a paper towel. Wear an apron and use a splatter screen to protect yourself.
- Place any pots or pans of hot liquid or oil on the back burner, and make sure all handles are turned inward, away from the front of the stove so that you don't bump them by mistake.
- Use only microwave-safe containers (never metals) in the microwave, and remove lids carefully to avoid burns.

Germy Things

- Before and after you cook, wash your hands for 20 seconds with soap and warm water to get rid of any germs. Always wash your hands with soapy water after touching raw meat and eggs and their packaging.
- Don't eat raw eggs. They may carry a type of bacteria called salmonella that can make you sick. No licking the batter spoon!
- Keep raw meats separate from other ingredients. If you use a board to cut raw meat, don't place your nonmeat ingredients on that board without thoroughly washing it first. And don't reuse tools used on raw meats with other foods.
- Don't leave any food out at room temperature for more than two hours (or one hour if the temperature is above 90°F). Always follow cooking times and temperatures to make sure your food is fully cooked.
- Clean as you go. Have a damp cloth nearby to wipe up spills or messes as you cook.

Smoked Turkey Sausage and Egg Hash PAGE 38

TOOLS YOU NEED

Get to know the tools you'll be using the most!

BAKING DISHES: These glass or ceramic dishes are for cooking food in the oven. They come in different sizes, depths, and shapes.

BAKING SHEETS: These flat, rectangular metal sheets are used for oven cooking. Rimmed sheets prevent drips.

BLENDER: This appliance used for mixing, blending, and pureeing. It's great for making sauces, dips, soups, and more.

BOX GRATER: Use this to shred cheese, vegetables, and other ingredients.

CHEF'S KNIFE: This knife has a broad blade that can be used for chopping, dicing, mincing, and slicing.

COLANDERS AND STRAINERS: Colanders are used to drain pasta, grains, and vegetables. Strainers have a handle and are made of fine mesh. Use a strainer when sifting flour or separating small amounts of liquid (such as broth) into a bowl.

COOKING THERMOMETER: A cooking thermometer measures the internal temperature of foods (primarily meats) in the oven so you know when they're finished cooking.

CUTTING BOARDS: These wood or vinyl boards are made for cutting your ingredients. A vinyl board, which is easy to clean, is great for beginners.

LADLE: Use a ladle to transfer hot liquids from a pot to a bowl.

LIQUID AND DRY MEASURING CUPS: Measuring cups for liquids have a spout so you can easily pour the ingredient. Dry measuring cups have flat edges so you can level the ingredient with the back of a knife.

MEASURING SPOONS: These plastic or metal spoons are used to measure dry or liquid ingredients and range in size from ⅛ teaspoon to 1 tablespoon.

MIXING BOWLS AND SPOONS: You'll want ceramic or glass mixing bowls of different sizes for combining ingredients. Metal spoons are used for mixing in a bowl, while a large wooden spoon is great for stirring at the stove.

MUFFIN TINS: These come in standard size (12 cups) and mini (24 small cups), and they are used to make baked goods and savory items.

PARING KNIFE: This short-bladed knife is used to cut, slice, and peel.

POTS: Available in different sizes, pots are used for making soups, stews, pastas, and more.

SAUCEPANS: These pans have straight sides and one long handle. They're used for boiling and simmering liquids and even for searing food (creating a browned crust at a high temperature).

SKILLETS: Pans with curved sides for sautéing, searing, and panfrying. Options include oven-safe, cast-iron, and nonstick.

SPATULAS: These are long-handled tools with an angled, flat surface to scrape, flip, and lift foods. They come in wood, silicone, plastic, or metal.

STAND OR HAND MIXER: This appliance is great for mixing batter, dough, frosting, and more. Ask an adult for help when you're learning how to use one.

TONGS: A pair of grippers used to lift and transfer (or serve) food. They're long, short, or forked, and some have silicone tips.

VEGETABLE PEELER: A tool used to remove the skin from fruits and vegetables.

WHISK: This wire-looped tool with a handle is used to blend ingredients and bring air into a mixture.

WIRE COOLING RACKS: These racks help air move freely to cool down baked goods.

WHAT TO KEEP HANDY

Now it's time to talk all about the good stuff—food. Some of these ingredients can be stored on kitchen shelves, while others need to be refrigerated. If you always have these in your kitchen, you'll always be ready to get your cook on!

BUTTER AND OILS: Butter is used in everyday cooking and baking, adding the fat needed for baked goods. Oils are helpful for frying, sautéing, and baking. I use canola oil for cooking and baking, but you can use any oil with a high smoke point (meaning it won't burn at high heat). Olive oil is excellent for marinades and dressings as well as for dipping. Store all oils in a cool, dark cabinet.

DAIRY: Rich in calcium, some of the milk products you'll use are cheese for sandwiches, yogurt for breakfast, and cream cheese for dips. You'll also be using milk for some of your dessert masterpieces.

EGGS: Used to make classic breakfasts, eggs are also important for everyday cooking and baking. Here's a tip for cracking eggs: Gently grip the egg and tap it against a clean cutting board or countertop until you hear a crack. Hold the egg over a bowl, use your thumbs to separate the eggshell at the crack, and tip the egg into the bowl. Voilà! Remember, wash your hands after handling raw eggs!

FRUITS: Adding flavor and nutrients, fruits can be used in both sweet and savory recipes. Always wash your fruit, and dry it well if you're cooking with it.

GRAINS: Made from wheat or other grains, foods like breads, pastas, and tortillas make meals hearty and satisfying. Flour is a must for baking, too!

MEAT: Meat, packed with protein, is so versatile. Chicken, beef, fish, and pork can be used in lots of recipes. Always wash your hands after handling any kind of raw meat.

NUTS: Use nuts to add crunch and texture to any dish. Chopped nuts can be a topping, a cookie mix-in, or blended into a spread. They're great to have on hand.

SEASONINGS: Salt and pepper flavor food. To enhance flavors even more, try fresh herbs, garlic and onion powder, chili powder, paprika, and barbecue sauce or soy sauce.

SUGAR: Use sugar to add sweetness to any dish. Make cookies, brownies, dips, and more with sugar. It's good to have granulated, brown, and confectioners' sugar on hand.

VEGETABLES: We all know veggies are rich in vitamins, but they also add flavor, color, and healthy fiber. Enjoy them in fajitas, salads, soups, salsas, and more. Always wash vegetables, and dry them well before cooking.

TOP 5 TIPS

Here are five more tips that the best cooks always keep in mind. Remember them, and you'll really up your cooking game!

1. **DON'T BE AFRAID TO ASK FOR HELP.** To be safe, let an adult know when you're going to cook, and ask for help when you need it. Make sure you understand how to safely use knives, stoves, and any other electric appliances.

2. **TAKE YOUR TIME.** Don't rush or try to do more than one thing at a time; that's when most mistakes and accidents happen. The more you practice cooking, the quicker you'll become.

3. **READ THE RECIPE—ONCE, TWICE, THREE TIMES.** Before you start cooking, read the recipe from beginning to end a couple of times. That way, you can be sure you have everything you need and know what you need to do.

4. **TASTE YOUR FOOD.** Add seasonings a little at a time and taste your food as you cook to make sure you're not overdoing it. It's easier to add seasoning than take it away.

5. **USE YOUR TIME WELL.** If you're waiting around for water to boil or for something to cook in the oven, wash your prep tools, put away ingredients, and wipe down your cooking station.

sweet and spicy Pork Tacos PAGE 78

CHAPTER 2

HOW TO GET COOKING

It's time to start cooking! In this chapter, you'll learn how to read a recipe, measure dry and wet ingredients, and discover different ways to mix, cut, and apply heat.

One of the most important things to do is to set up everything you need on the counter. This is what chefs call *mise en place*, a French expression for "putting everything in place." You'll want to gather all the equipment and utensils you'll need and prep and place the ingredients in the order you'll use them.

Veggie Ramen with "Jammy" Eggs PAGE 76

HOW TO READ A RECIPE

A recipe is like a map to good food, guiding you step-by-step to your destination. You read (and reread) the recipe first to find out which tools and ingredients you need and what steps are listed in the instructions. If there's anything you don't understand, ask an adult. Then follow the instructions carefully.

As you make your way through the fun, delicious recipes in this book, you'll notice labels below each recipe's title that will help you understand what to expect or see if you have enough time or ingredients to complete a recipe. The labels will also let you know if the recipe is free of certain ingredients (such as nuts or meat). Pretty useful, huh?

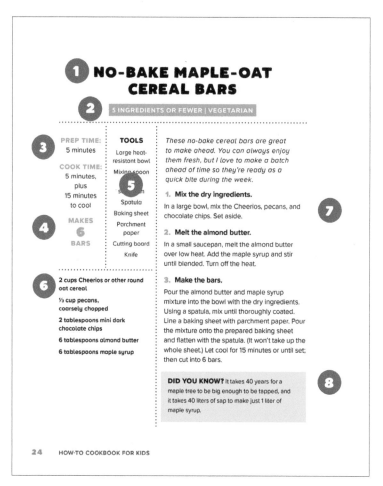

① NO-BAKE MAPLE-OAT CEREAL BARS

② 5 INGREDIENTS OR FEWER | VEGETARIAN

③ **PREP TIME:**
5 minutes

COOK TIME:
5 minutes, plus 15 minutes to cool

④ **MAKES**
6
BARS

TOOLS
Large heat-resistant bowl
Mixing spoon
⑤ Saucepan
Spatula
Baking sheet
Parchment paper
Cutting board
Knife

⑥ 2 cups Cheerios or other round oat cereal

⅓ cup pecans, coarsely chopped

2 tablespoons mini dark chocolate chips

6 tablespoons almond butter

6 tablespoons maple syrup

These no-bake cereal bars are great to make ahead. You can always enjoy them fresh, but I love to make a batch ahead of time so they're ready as a quick bite during the week.

1. Mix the dry ingredients.

⑦ In a large bowl, mix the Cheerios, pecans, and chocolate chips. Set aside.

2. Melt the almond butter.

In a small saucepan, melt the almond butter over low heat. Add the maple syrup and stir until blended. Turn off the heat.

3. Make the bars.

Pour the almond butter and maple syrup mixture into the bowl with the dry ingredients. Using a spatula, mix until thoroughly coated. Line a baking sheet with parchment paper. Pour the mixture onto the prepared baking sheet and flatten with the spatula. (It won't take up the whole sheet.) Let cool for 15 minutes or until set; then cut into 6 bars.

⑧ **DID YOU KNOW?** It takes 40 years for a maple tree to be big enough to be tapped, and it takes 40 liters of sap to make just 1 liter of maple syrup.

1. **TITLE:** The title tells you what the recipe is. It usually showcases a standout flavor or ingredient and lets you know what to expect.

2. **RECIPE LABELS:** Labels give you specific, helpful information about the recipe. The labels you'll see in this book are:

   No Heat Necessary: These meals require no heating whatsoever before getting to the deliciousness. You'll assemble, mix, or blend ingredients together. Sometimes chilling in the refrigerator is needed.

   5 Ingredients or Fewer: These recipes use only five ingredients or fewer (not counting the standard salt, pepper, water, and oil).

   Fast: If you're low on time, these recipes are under 10 minutes to make!

   No Nuts: If you're cooking for someone who has a nut restriction, this label marks nut-free recipes that are safe to enjoy.

   Vegetarian: These recipes do not contain meat.

   Vegan: These recipes do not contain meat, dairy, or eggs.

3. **PREP TIME AND COOK TIME:** Prep time is how long you'll spend preparing the ingredients. Cook time is how long the food will be in the oven or on the stovetop.

4. **YIELD:** This line tells you how many people the recipe will feed ("Serves 8") or how much it makes ("Makes 12 cookies").

5. **TOOLS:** This list provides all the equipment and tools you'll need to prepare the recipe.

6. **INGREDIENTS:** Read this list carefully, both to make sure you have everything, and because sometimes it includes prep directions. (For example, "1 carrot, peeled and diced" means you need to do this beforehand.)

7. **METHOD:** These step-by-step instructions walk you through preparing, cooking, and assembling the meal.

8. **RECIPE TIPS:** Many recipes end with helpful and fun information about ingredients as well as suggestions for how to change up a recipe.

This book includes the following tips:

Don't Have It? Suggestions for ingredient substitutions.

Another Idea: How to take the recipe up a notch, either with a more challenging technique or by adding a little something extra to the final dish.

Helpful Hint: Tips for making sure the recipes comes out right.

Store It: Information about how to store leftovers.

Did You Know? Fun facts about ingredients.

MEASURE IT

Every recipe calls for different, specific measurements. Mixing and measuring may seem simple, but they're actually two of the most important skills to master. Being precise means getting consistent results. Practice makes perfect, and the more you do it, the more you'll find yourself getting comfortable with these skills.

Measuring Dry Ingredients

How to measure dry ingredients 1

How to measure dry ingredients 2

Dry ingredients include things like flour, sugar, oats, salt, baking soda, baking powder, and yeast. To measure dry ingredients, use measuring spoons or dry measuring cups (which often come in nested sets). The easiest way to measure dry ingredients is to use the "scoop and scrape" method. Using the spoon or cup, scoop up the dry ingredient and fill it just past the top; then use your finger or the flat part of a butter knife and scrape across the top to level it.

Measuring Wet Ingredients

Water, milk, oil, melted butter, eggs, and applesauce are examples of wet ingredients. To measure small amounts of liquids, hold a measuring spoon level over a plate or bowl and pour in the liquid until you fill the spoon. (You can scoop thicker ingredients like peanut butter.) For larger quantities, place a liquid measuring cup (which often has a spout) on the countertop and pour in your liquid until it reaches the right line (such as the one marking "¼ cup," "½ cup," or "1 cup").

How to measure wet ingredients 1

How to measure wet ingredients 2

MIX IT

When you read a recipe, you'll notice words like *stir, mix, fold, whisk, toss,* and *puree.* These are different techniques used to combine ingredients.

STIR: Stirring is when you move a utensil like a spoon or a spatula in a circular motion to create a mixture, disperse heat, or make a sauce thicker or thinner.

MIX: Mixing is when you combine two or more ingredients. For example, you would mix ground spices together in a bowl to make a spice rub. You can mix ingredients using a spoon, a whisk, a fork, or even your hands.

FOLD: Folding means to carefully combine two ingredients or mixtures that are different in weight into one smooth mixture. You can do this by using a large metal spoon or silicone spatula to lift both ingredients together and turn them over so they combine.

WHISK: Whisking means to stir something with light but quick movements, usually using a whisk or a fork. This technique helps you smoothly blend a mixture or add air into it (often done with eggs to make them fluffy).

How to mix

How to whisk

How to fold 1

How to fold 2

TOSS: Tossing means to mix ingredients together by lightly lifting and turning them. This technique is usually used to evenly coat ingredients in a sauce or seasoning mix without bruising or mashing them. For example, you might toss a salad, a snack mix, or a pasta dish.

PUREE: Pureeing creates a smooth paste or liquid (with a pudding-like texture) by pressing cooked ingredients through a mesh strainer or blending them in a blender.

CUT IT

You may notice words like *slice, chop, dice*, and *mince* in recipes. These terms describe how to use your knife to cut your ingredients. Make sure you've read the safety tips on page 2.

Different knives do different things. Serrated knives (with saw-like teeth on the blade) work better for cutting foods with soft centers, while paring knives can help core strawberries or handle other small tasks. A chef's knife is a good knife to start with. It can do most of the cutting you'll need for fruit, vegetables, and meats.

SLICE: To cut food into thin or thick uniformly sized pieces. To slice, place the ingredient on its side and hold it firmly but gently with your guide hand using a claw grip (see page 2). Use a careful sawing motion with your knife and work the blade down from top to bottom to make a full slice.

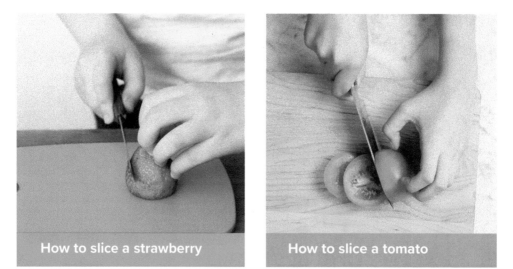

How to slice a strawberry

How to slice a tomato

HALVE: To cut into two equal portions. You can do this with many fruits and vegetables as well as some meats. Use a claw grip and hold down the ingredient on a cutting board. Place the blade in the middle of the food. With a careful sawing motion, slice all the way through.

CHOP: To cut into bite-size pieces (about ¼ inch). Set the ingredient on a cutting board so the long side is flat against the board. Slice into it lengthwise to create planks. Lay down a plank flat, and slice it into three pieces lengthwise. Quarter-turn the pieces and cut them into cubes crosswise. Repeat with the rest of the planks. When a recipe calls for food to be "finely chopped," you can cut the pieces smaller, to about ⅛ inch. And if it says "coarsely chopped," the chunks can be larger.

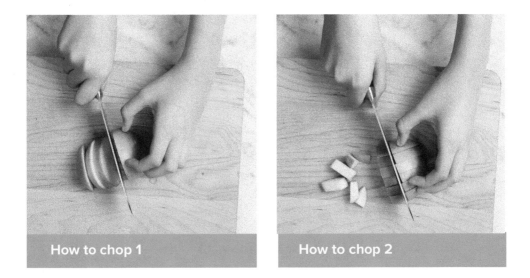

How to chop 1   How to chop 2

DICE: To cut into pieces that are smaller, neater, and more uniform in size than chopping. Slice the ingredient in half. Place a half cut-side down on the cutting board so the side is facing you; then grip with your guide hand. Make two horizontal slices without cutting all the way through. Turn the food so the top end is facing you and make vertical cuts across it. Turn it back so the side is facing you again. Slice into the ingredient crosswise all the way through. ("Cubed" has a similar meaning to diced, but the pieces are larger, about ½ inch.)

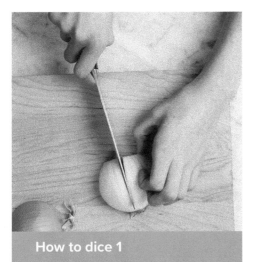

How to dice 1

How to dice 2

MINCE: To use the finest level of chopping. Minced foods are mostly used for seasoning. This cut helps distribute ingredients evenly and enhances the flavor in recipes. To mince, firmly grip the knife handle and place your guide hand on top of the blade. Use the claw grip and slice the ingredient lengthwise. Turn it, and then slice it crosswise.

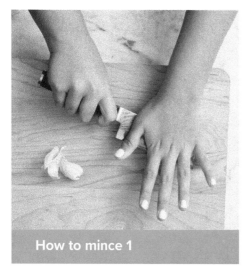

How to mince 1

How to mince 2

GRATE: To turn food into tiny shreds by rubbing it against a grater. Firmly hold down the grater against a cutting board. Using your dominant hand, start slowly, and be cautious with your knuckles. Press the ingredient against the grater, and apply pressure on the downward stroke only.

How to grate

HEAT IT

There are many ways to cook using a stovetop and oven. Get to know these methods—you'll see them throughout this book.

Remember to always let an adult know when you're using the stove or oven, stay in the kitchen while you're cooking, and follow the precautions on pages 2 and 3 for safety.

BOIL: To cook food at a high temperature in water or some other water-based liquid. (The boiling point of water is 212°F.) Fill a pot three-quarters full, cover, and set the stove to high heat to achieve a rolling boil (large bursting bubbles rising to the top); reduce heat to medium-low to thicken a liquid to a sauce. Sometimes, you'll see instructions to bring a liquid up to a roiling or medium boil before turning the heat down to a simmer. To simmer, keep the heat on low.

SAUTÉ: To cook small or thin pieces of food in a hot pan with butter or oil. It's essential to use high heat. Once the pan is hot, add oil or butter. Add your food when the oil is hot. Shake the pan (or use a heat-resistant spatula) to cook your food evenly.

PANFRY: To cook larger pieces of food. The results are juicy yet browned and crispy. The food isn't fully covered by oil, and you will have to turn it at least once. Keep the stove on medium-high, heat the oil, place the food in the pan, and cook for each side's required time.

BAKE: To surround food with dry heat in the oven. It gently cooks and tenderizes savory food. When making desserts, baking makes the batter or dough rise and form a crust—kind of like edible science!

ABOUT THE RECIPES

The recipes in this book will use the methods and tools you've learned about in this section. Each of the following chapters will teach you how to make dishes for a specific meal or kind of recipe, from sweet and savory breakfasts to satisfying main courses to super-yummy desserts. Have fun, and be sure to ask an adult if you have any questions!

CHAPTER 3

HOW TO MAKE BREAKFAST

Buttermilk Waffles with Maple Syrup PAGE 32

NO-BAKE MAPLE-OAT CEREAL BARS

5 INGREDIENTS OR FEWER | VEGETARIAN

PREP TIME:
5 minutes

COOK TIME:
5 minutes,
plus
15 minutes
to cool

MAKES
6
BARS

TOOLS

Large heat-resistant bowl

Mixing spoon

Small saucepan

Spatula

Baking sheet

Parchment paper

Cutting board

Knife

2 cups Cheerios or other round oat cereal

⅓ cup pecans, coarsely chopped

2 tablespoons mini dark chocolate chips

6 tablespoons almond butter

6 tablespoons maple syrup

These no-bake cereal bars are great to make ahead. You can always enjoy them fresh, but I love to make a batch ahead of time so they're ready as a quick bite during the week.

1. Mix the dry ingredients.

In a large bowl, mix the Cheerios, pecans, and chocolate chips. Set aside.

2. Melt the almond butter.

In a small saucepan, melt the almond butter over low heat. Add the maple syrup and stir until blended. Turn off the heat.

3. Make the bars.

Pour the almond butter and maple syrup mixture into the bowl with the dry ingredients. Using a spatula, mix until thoroughly coated. Line a baking sheet with parchment paper. Pour the mixture onto the prepared baking sheet and flatten with the spatula. (It won't take up the whole sheet.) Let cool for 15 minutes or until set; then cut into 6 bars.

DID YOU KNOW? It takes 40 years for a maple tree to be big enough to be tapped, and it takes 40 liters of sap to make just 1 liter of maple syrup.

STRAWBERRIES AND CREAM OATMEAL

NO NUTS | VEGETARIAN

TOOLS

Medium saucepan

Mixing spoon

Blender

Wooden spoon

1½ cups rolled oats

Pinch salt

1 cup whole milk

1 cup water

2 cups roughly chopped strawberries, plus ⅓ cup diced strawberries

½ tablespoon vanilla extract

¼ cup maple syrup, plus more for serving

ANOTHER IDEA: For a little extra yumminess, you can top the oatmeal with chia seeds, sliced bananas, dark chocolate chunks, or coconut chips. Change the flavor by replacing the strawberries with peaches. Peaches and cream oatmeal? Yes, please!

Oatmeal is hearty, packed with fiber, and so satisfying. This oatmeal is incredibly creamy and filled with delicious strawberries.

1. Prepare the oats.

In an unheated medium saucepan, combine the rolled oats and salt, stir, and set aside.

2. Make the strawberry cream.

Combine the milk, water, 2 cups of roughly chopped strawberries, vanilla, and maple syrup in a blender pitcher. Ask an adult to show you how to use the blender, and blend until smooth. (Follow blender safety tips—never place your hand in a blender.)

3. Combine and cook the oats.

With your saucepan on the stove, set the heat to medium and pour the strawberry cream into the mixture of rolled oats and salt. Stir until thoroughly combined. Using a wooden spoon, stir frequently for 10 to 15 minutes, or until the oatmeal thickens. Once thickened, stir in ⅓ cup of diced strawberries, remove from the heat, and spoon into bowls. Drizzle some of the maple syrup onto the oatmeal in each bowl and serve.

BREAKFAST BANANA SPLIT

5 INGREDIENTS OR FEWER | FAST | NO HEAT NECESSARY | VEGETARIAN

PREP TIME:
10 minutes

SERVES
2

TOOLS

Cutting board

Knife

Small bowl

2 plates

Spoon

½ cup roasted, shelled peanuts

2 bananas

½ cup vanilla Greek yogurt, divided

4 tablespoons cherry jam, divided

½ cup blueberries, divided

Having ice cream for breakfast is the dream, right? This take on the familiar banana split is pretty epic in its own right. Topped with delicious but better-for-you ingredients, this dish will give you plenty of energy to take on the day!

1. Chop the peanuts.

On a cutting board, coarsely chop the peanuts; then place them in a small bowl.

2. Split the bananas.

Peel the bananas and cut about 1 inch off both ends. Cut the bananas in half lengthwise. Arranging one banana per plate, place the two halves in the center so they curve away from each other.

3. Top the banana splits.

Spoon half the yogurt across the banana halves. Top evenly with 2 tablespoons of cherry jam. Sprinkle half the blueberries over the banana and finish by topping with half the chopped peanuts. Repeat with the remaining banana.

ANOTHER IDEA: You can also add chocolate chips, granola, coconut, peanut butter, honey, all kinds of fruit—the choice is yours.

TROPICAL SMOOTHIE BOWL

NO HEAT NECESSARY | FAST | VEGAN

PREP TIME:
10 minutes

SERVES
2

TOOLS

Blender

Wooden spoon
or spatula

Cutting board

Knife

2 small bowls

Vegetable
peeler

1 sliced and frozen banana

1 cup frozen pineapple chunks

1 cup frozen mango chunks

1 cup coconut milk, plus more
if needed

2 kiwis

⅓ cup almonds

⅓ cup fresh blueberries

⅓ cup coconut chips

¼ cup chia seeds

ANOTHER IDEA: Make
it hot pink! Add unique color
and flavor by adding pitaya,
also known as dragon fruit.

*Take a trip to the tropics with this
smoothie bowl. Keep resealable bags of
the chopped fruit in the freezer so you
can whip one up anytime. If you don't
have frozen fruit at the ready, just add
1½ cups of ice.*

1. Blend and pour the smoothies.

In a blender, pulse to blend the banana, pineapple, mango, and coconut milk until smooth.
Stop occasionally to stir with a wooden spoon.
If the blend is too thick to pulse, add a little
more coconut milk. The mixture should be
thicker than a regular smoothie. Pour into
two bowls.

2. Slice the kiwis and chop the almonds.

On a cutting board, peel the kiwis and slice
into rounds. Coarsely chop the almonds and
set aside.

3. Make the bowls.

Get creative and make your smoothie bowl
shine. Top your vibrant canvas (the smoothie
base) with the kiwis, almonds, blueberries,
coconut chips, and chia seeds. Use them to
create stripes or other patterns across the
smoothie bowls.

BREAKFAST TACOS WITH QUESO FRESCO

`NO NUTS`

PREP TIME:
10 minutes

COOK TIME:
25 minutes

**SERVES 2
(4 TACOS
EACH)**

TOOLS

Large skillet

Cutting board

Knife

Spatula

Plate

Paper towel

1 tablespoon extra-virgin olive oil

1 medium potato (Yukon Gold preferred), washed and cubed

¼ teaspoon garlic powder

⅛ teaspoon red pepper flakes

½ teaspoon salt

⅛ teaspoon black pepper

¼ cup chopped onion

1 (10-ounce) pork chorizo link

4 eggs

8 (4.5-inch) corn tortillas

½ cup queso fresco, crumbled

Every day is Taco Tuesday in my heart. These mini breakfast tacos are so full of flavor, with chorizo (a type of sausage) and Mexican queso fresco, which means "fresh cheese." Similar to feta cheese, queso fresco is crumbly, creamy, and a little bit salty. Make these vegetarian by using mushrooms instead of chorizo.

1. Cook the potato and onion.

In a large skillet, heat the oil over medium-high heat. Add the cubed potato, garlic powder, red pepper flakes, salt, pepper, and onion and cook for 10 minutes, or until cooked through.

2. Add the chorizo and eggs.

Using a knife, carefully cut the chorizo lengthwise and remove the casing. Crumble into the skillet and cook for 5 minutes. Crack the eggs into the mixture and let cook for 30 seconds; then gently stir for 5 minutes, or until cooked through and the filling is well combined.

3. Warm the tortillas, fill, and enjoy.

Place the tortillas in a stack on a plate and cover them with a damp paper towel. Microwave on high for 30 to 60 seconds, until warm and soft. Fill each tortilla with the taco filling. Top with queso fresco.

FLUFFY SCRAMBLED EGGS WITH CHEESE

5 INGREDIENTS OR FEWER | FAST | VEGETARIAN

PREP TIME:
2 minutes

COOK TIME:
8 minutes

SERVES
4

TOOLS

Medium bowl

Whisk

Large nonstick pan

Spatula

8 large eggs

2 tablespoons whole milk

⅛ teaspoon salt

Pinch black pepper

2 tablespoons unsalted butter

½ cup shredded cheddar cheese

A tasty start to any day, scrambled eggs are a crowd-pleaser on their own and also give you lots of room to be creative. Once you know how to make them, you can add different toppings like diced tomatoes, cubed ham, crumbled bacon, and fresh chives.

1. Prepare the egg mixture.

Break the eggs into a medium bowl. Add the milk, salt, and pepper, and whisk briskly for 60 seconds until combined.

2. Heat and butter the pan.

Heat a large nonstick pan on medium-low heat. Use a spatula to place the butter in the pan. (Do not touch the surface or sides of the pan with your hands. Only use the handle.) Spread the melting butter with a spatula to coat the pan.

DON'T HAVE IT? If you don't have milk, use 2 tablespoons of cream or half-and-half. Don't like the taste of milk or have an allergy to it? Use water instead.

3. **Cook the eggs.**

Keep the heat on medium-low. (If the heat is too high, the eggs will cook too quickly, and the texture will change.) Pour the egg mixture into the pan. Take your spatula with your dominant hand, hold the handle of the pan with your other hand, and fold the outer edges of the egg mixture, which is beginning to cook, into the center of the pan. You'll notice the uncooked egg mixture will flood the area you just folded in. Keep folding in until there's no longer any uncooked egg mixture. Break up the scramble with your spatula and keep it moving so it doesn't overcook. Once the eggs are moist (not runny), stir in the cheddar cheese, turn off the heat, and serve immediately.

BUTTERMILK WAFFLES WITH MAPLE SYRUP

PREP TIME:
5 minutes

COOK TIME:
20 minutes

SERVES
4

TOOLS

Waffle maker

Large bowl

Whisk

Fork

Mixing spoon

Silicone spatula

Nonstick cooking spray (optional)

1¾ cup all-purpose flour

2 teaspoons baking powder

½ teaspoon salt

1 tablespoon granulated sugar

3 large eggs

7 tablespoons vegetable oil

1½ cups buttermilk

1 teaspoon vanilla extract

Powdered sugar, for topping

Maple syrup, for topping

You'll need to use an electric waffle maker for this recipe, so check with an adult first. Waffles are really fun to make, and you can mix in different fruits or chocolate or add almost any topping your heart desires! You can even top them with savory ingredients.

1. Preheat and grease the waffle maker.

Set the waffle maker to medium-high. Lightly spray both metal plates with nonstick cooking spray (if using).

2. Make the waffle batter.

In a large bowl, whisk together the flour, baking powder, salt, and sugar. Make a well in the middle of your dry ingredients. (A well is a hole or space where you will add a liquid.) Break the eggs into the well and use a fork to lightly beat the eggs until they break apart. Add the oil, buttermilk, and vanilla and stir the whole bowl well, until combined. If you have a few lumps, that's okay, as long as the batter is moist.

HELPFUL HINT: While you're making the waffles, you might think to stack them. That often leaves your waffles soggy by the time you're ready to serve. Instead, set your oven or toaster oven to 200°F and place the waffles onto the rack for 3 to 5 minutes. This extra step makes the waffles crispy on the outside and fluffy on the inside.

3. Cook the waffles.

Spoon ½ cup of the batter into the hot waffle maker and close the lid. As your waffle cooks, it will release steam. Cook for about 5 minutes or until your waffle maker tells you it's done; the waffle should be golden brown and crispy. Another hint: Once the steam stops coming out from the sides, your waffle should be ready! Using a spatula, remove the waffle from the waffle maker. Repeat these steps until you run out of batter. Place the waffles on plates, sprinkle with powdered sugar, and drizzle with maple syrup.

PERFECTLY FLUFFY BLUEBERRY PANCAKES

PREP TIME:
5 minutes

COOK TIME:
20 minutes

SERVES
4

TOOLS

Large bowl

Whisk

Butter knife

Small microwave-safe dish

Medium bowl

Spoon

Large skillet

Ladle

Spatula

1 cup all-purpose flour

2 tablespoons granulated sugar

2 teaspoons baking powder

½ teaspoon salt

4 tablespoons butter, divided, plus more for serving

1 cup room-temperature milk

1 large egg

1 cup fresh or frozen blueberries

Maple syrup, for topping

Pancakes are a breakfast staple. They're great for a group, and you can change the mix-ins and toppings up with different fruits, brown butter (butter that's browned in a pan), cinnamon, chocolate—the possibilities are endless!

1. **Prepare the dry ingredients.**

In a large bowl, whisk together the flour, sugar, baking powder, and salt, and set aside.

2. **Melt the butter and combine the wet and dry ingredients.**

Cut 2 tablespoons of the butter into small pieces and place them in a microwave-safe dish. Microwave, uncovered, for 30 seconds on high. Continue in 10-second increments until melted. In a medium bowl, whisk together the room-temperature milk, melted butter, and egg. Add the mixture to the dry ingredients and mix until just combined. If using fresh blueberries, add them. Do not stir the batter too much, since overmixing can make pancakes heavy and flat. If you're using frozen blueberries, don't add them directly into the batter. Instead, add the frozen berries after you start cooking the pancakes in the next step; you'll put them directly into the uncooked sides of the pancakes in the skillet before you flip them.

3. Cook the pancakes and serve.

In a large skillet, melt the remaining 2 tablespoons of butter over medium heat. When the butter is melted, reduce the heat to low and ladle in the batter, about ¼ cup per pancake. Once the pancakes start forming bubbles, flip and cook until the other side is golden brown (usually 1 to 2 minutes per side). It's always best to lift the bottom of the pancake partway with a spatula and see how it looks before flipping. Once the pancake is cooked on both sides, remove and repeat with the remaining batter. Turn off the heat and serve the pancakes, topping them with butter and drizzling with maple syrup.

"JAMMY" EGGS WITH BACON

NO NUTS

PREP TIME:
3 minutes

COOK TIME:
20 minutes,
5 minutes
to cool

SERVES
4

TOOLS

Skillet

Tongs

Plate with
paper towels
on top

Cutting board

Knife

Small bowl

Whisk

Medium bowl

Medium
saucepan

Slotted spoon

4 slices bacon

½ cup mayonnaise

½ teaspoon fresh or
dried parsley

1 teaspoon lemon juice

1 teaspoon minced garlic

1 teaspoon
Worcestershire sauce

8 large eggs

Salt

"Jammy" eggs mean the yolk is cooked to be soft and creamy. But once you know how to boil eggs, you can make them firmer or softer if you prefer. This recipe has a soft yolk, and it is packed with flavor, thanks to a crispy bacon topping and a garlic aioli, a French name for a mayonnaise-based sauce.

1. Cook and chop the bacon.

Place the bacon in one layer on a cold skillet and cook over low heat for 8 to 12 minutes. Once the bacon starts to brown and release its fat, flip it with tongs and fry until browned. Turn off the heat, remove the pan from the hot part of the stove, and use tongs to lift the bacon and move it to a plate lined with paper towels. Let the bacon cool for 5 minutes. Place the cooled bacon on a cutting board, coarsely chop it, and set aside.

2. Make the garlic aioli sauce.

In a small bowl, whisk together the mayonnaise, parsley, lemon juice, garlic, and Worcestershire sauce until combined. Set aside.

3. Cook the eggs.

Fill a medium bowl with cold water and ice and set aside. (Once your eggs are boiled, you'll put them in this cold-water bath to stop them from cooking further.) Bring a saucepan of water to a rolling boil on high heat. Make sure you have enough water to cover the eggs by 1 inch. Once the water is boiling, reduce the heat (so the eggs won't bounce around and break). Add the eggs to the water and cover the pot for 6 minutes. (If you don't like jammy eggs, you can set the timer for 9 minutes for a slightly firmer soft yolk or 10 to 13 minutes for a firm yolk.) Turn off the heat and use a slotted spoon to transfer the eggs to the bowl of ice water. After about 2 minutes, remove them from the water. On a clean, flat surface, tap an egg hard once to break the shell and roll it with your hand to peel it. You can also tap on the egg base to crack it and run it under cold water to peel. Cut the eggs in half lengthwise, sprinkle with salt, top with ½ teaspoon of garlic aioli, add the chopped bacon, and serve.

SMOKED TURKEY SAUSAGE AND EGG HASH

5 INGREDIENTS OR FEWER | NO NUTS

PREP TIME:
10 minutes

COOK TIME:
30 minutes

SERVES
4

TOOLS

Large oven-safe skillet with lid

Wooden spoon

Small bowl

2 tablespoons extra-virgin olive oil

4 medium potatoes (Yukon Gold preferred), cleaned, peeled, and diced

¾ cup smoked turkey sausage, skinless and cubed

½ teaspoon salt, plus more as needed

½ teaspoon black pepper, plus more as needed

⅓ cup shredded cheddar cheese

4 large eggs

2 green onions, trimmed and finely chopped

To make this hearty breakfast, potatoes, turkey sausage, gooey cheese, eggs, and flavorful green onions are all cooked in one skillet. I love serving it in the skillet, too, because it looks so impressive.

1. Preheat the oven.

Preheat the oven to 400°F.

2. Cook the potatoes.

In a large oven-safe skillet, heat the oil over medium heat. Add the potatoes and fry for 20 minutes, stirring every 5 minutes or so, until cooked through. Speed up the cooking time by covering the skillet. In the last 5 minutes, add the turkey sausage, salt, and pepper, and stir to combine.

3. Add the cheese, eggs, and green onions.

Sprinkle the cheese all over the hash. Use a wooden spoon to make four evenly spaced wells in the hash. Crack an egg into a bowl (keeping the yolk whole) and pour it into one of the wells; pour one egg into each well. Cover the skillet, place it in the oven, and bake for about 10 minutes, until the egg whites are set. Remove from the oven and sprinkle with the chopped green onions and salt and pepper to taste.

ANOTHER IDEA: To make this dish vegetarian, replace the turkey sausage with cubed tempeh or portabella mushrooms. You can also replace some or all of the potatoes with sweet potatoes.

HOW TO MAKE SNACKS AND SIDES

Crispy Chicken Tenders with Secret Sauce PAGE 52

BAKED PARMESAN-GARLIC TORTILLA CHIPS

5 INGREDIENTS OR FEWER | NO NUTS | VEGETARIAN

PREP TIME:
10 minutes

COOK TIME:
10 minutes

MAKES
3
CUPS, OR
32
CHIPS

TOOLS

Large baking sheet

Parchment paper

Cutting board

Knife

Small bowl

Fork

Basting brush

Tongs

4 (8-inch) flour tortillas

⅓ cup extra-virgin olive oil

2 tablespoons grated Parmesan cheese

1 tablespoon garlic powder

1 teaspoon dried parsley

⅛ teaspoon salt

⅛ teaspoon black pepper

Not only are these homemade chips fresh, crispy, and flavorful, but they're also healthier than store-bought. Serve with salsa, guacamole, or creamy spinach dip.

1. Prepare the oven and baking sheet.

Preheat the oven to 425°F. Line a baking sheet with parchment paper and set aside.

2. Cut the tortillas into wedges.

Cut the tortillas into eighths by cutting first into quarters and then cutting each quarter in half.

3. Make the Parmesan-garlic oil.

In a small bowl, use a fork to whisk together the oil, cheese, garlic powder, parsley, salt, and pepper until well combined.

4. Bake the chips.

Place the tortilla wedges in a single layer on the baking sheet. Use a basting brush to paint the wedges with the Parmesan-garlic oil. Flip the tortilla wedges with the tongs and baste the other side. Bake for 10 minutes.

ANOTHER IDEA: Add nacho flavor with 1 teaspoon each of paprika and chili powder, or make them sweet by replacing the spices with ½ teaspoon of cinnamon and ¼ cup of sugar.

SWEET AND SPICY MANGO SALSA

NO HEAT NECESSARY | 5 INGREDIENTS OR FEWER | NO NUTS | VEGAN

PREP TIME:
20 minutes

MAKES
3
CUPS

TOOLS
Cutting board
Knife
Spoon
Medium bowl
Mixing spoon

3 medium mangos

1 small red onion, finely diced

1 jalapeño, seeded and finely minced

⅓ cup cilantro, finely chopped

Juice of one lime

½ teaspoon salt

⅛ teaspoon black pepper

DID YOU KNOW? In some Latin American countries, unripe, sour mangos are dipped in a mixture of salt, pepper, chili powder, and lime and eaten raw. Many people in El Salvador sprinkle the green mangos with lime and chili powder.

How can you make spicy salsa for chip dipping even better? Add some sweet mango! This recipe will keep in the refrigerator in an airtight container for up to 3 days.

1. Halve the mango.

Lay the mango on its side, securing it with the claw grip at the center of the fruit. Cut down lengthwise until you feel the pit and then cut around it. Turn the mango around and repeat. You should have two halves. Pull them apart and remove the pit. Repeat these steps with the remaining mangos.

2. Cut the mangos into cubes.

Cut ½-inch lines lengthwise through one half of the mango, but do not slice through to the skin. Do the same thing crosswise so you form a cubed pattern. Use a spoon to scoop the cubes away from the skin. Repeat with the remaining halves.

3. Mix the salsa and serve.

Place the cubed mangos, onion, jalapeño, cilantro, and lime juice in a medium bowl. Add the salt and pepper. With a mixing spoon, carefully toss together the salsa and serve.

KNOCKOUT GUACAMOLE

NO HEAT NECESSARY | 5 INGREDIENTS OR FEWER | FAST | NO NUTS | VEGAN

PREP TIME:
10 minutes

SERVES
4

TOOLS

Cutting board

Knife

Spoon

Butter knife

Medium bowl

Fork

3 ripe avocados

¼ teaspoon salt, plus more for seasoning

1 teaspoon lime juice

2 tablespoons red onion, finely chopped

1 tablespoon fresh cilantro, finely chopped (optional)

½ ripe tomato, chopped

black pepper

STORE IT: Place leftover guacamole in an airtight container. Pack it down tightly with a spoon. Add a thin layer (½ inch) of lukewarm water on top and seal with the lid. You can refrigerate it for up to 3 days. When you are ready to eat it, gently drain the water, stir, and enjoy.

Avocados, which are firm yet soft to the touch when ripe, are nature's butter, and guacamole makes use of avocados so well. It's creamy, savory, and great to pair with tortilla chips or as a side to your favorite Mexican dishes. Do you find that cilantro tastes funny? That's okay: about 14 percent of people do, and that's why it's optional to add in this guac!

1. Cut the avocados.

Cut one avocado lengthwise around the seed. Open the two halves and use a spoon to remove the pit. Use a butter knife to score (slice) the avocado lengthwise and crosswise without cutting through the peel. Spoon out the flesh of the avocado into a medium bowl. Repeat this process for all the avocados.

2. Mash and season the avocados.

In the medium bowl, use a fork to mash the avocados roughly. Try not to over-mash; this guacamole should have chunks. Add the salt, lime juice, red onion, cilantro (if using), tomato, and a pinch of pepper. Taste for salt and pepper and adjust to your preference. Mix until combined and serve immediately.

CHEESY QUESADILLA WITH ZESTY SOUR CREAM

NO NUTS | 5 INGREDIENTS OR FEWER | VEGETARIAN

PREP TIME:
5 minutes

COOK TIME:
20 minutes

SERVES
4

TOOLS

Small bowl

Mixing spoon

Large nonstick skillet

Spatula

Knife

1 cup sour cream

½ teaspoon chili powder

1 teaspoon seasoning salt

4 (6-inch) flour tortillas

2 cups shredded cheddar cheese

1 tomato, diced

2 tablespoons canola oil

ANOTHER IDEA: Add leftover taco meat and black beans with the cheese and tomatoes. Don't forget a side of guac!

This quesadilla is melty, crispy, and filled with juicy tomatoes. Serve with a lightly spiced sour cream to dip, and you have a quick and easy lunch. Once you know how to make a cheese quesadilla, you can add different fillings like chicken, ground beef, beans, corn, and more!

1. **Prepare the zesty sour cream.**

In a small bowl, mix the sour cream, chili powder, and seasoning salt until combined. Set aside.

2. **Prepare the quesadillas.**

Microwave the tortillas for 10 seconds. Lay them flat and top one side of each tortilla with cheese and tomatoes. Fold each tortilla over into a taco shape.

3. **Fry the quesadillas and serve.**

Heat the oil in a large nonstick skillet over medium heat. Place one of the folded tortillas into the skillet and fry for 2 minutes on each side. Use the spatula to press down on each side while it cooks. Repeat this process for all the tortillas. Turn off the heat, cut the quesadillas into three pieces, and serve with the zesty sour cream.

MINI PEPPERONI PIZZA QUICHES

NO NUTS

PREP TIME:
10 minutes

COOK TIME:
15 minutes,
plus
5 minutes
to cool

MAKES
24
QUICHES

TOOLS

24-cup mini
muffin tin

Medium bowl

Whisk

Large
measuring cup

Nonstick cooking spray

6 eggs

3 tablespoons milk

¼ cup chopped pepperoni

½ small red bell pepper, diced

½ small white onion, diced

1 teaspoon garlic powder

⅛ teaspoon dried parsley

½ teaspoon salt

1 cup shredded Colby Jack cheese

Pizza sauce, for dipping (optional)

Sometimes all I want is pizza, but making a whole pizza isn't always an option. These little pepperoni-top quiches give you a pizza fix anytime of the day.

1. Prepare the oven and muffin tin.

Preheat the oven to 350°F. Grease a muffin tin with cooking spray and set aside.

2. Prepare the egg mixture.

In a medium bowl, whisk together the eggs and milk until blended. Add the pepperoni, bell pepper, onion, garlic powder, parsley, and salt. Whisk until combined.

3. Portion the egg mixture and bake.

Transfer the egg mixture to a measuring cup; then carefully pour it into the muffin cups, stirring often and dividing evenly. Top with the cheese and bake for 15 minutes, or until the eggs are set. Remove from the oven and let cool for 5 minutes. Enjoy the quiches warm with pizza sauce on the side (if using).

STORE IT: Made too many or want to make ahead? Place cooled quiches in an airtight container and store in the refrigerator for 3 to 4 days.

CRISPY OVEN-BAKED FRIES WITH CHEESE SAUCE

NO NUTS | VEGETARIAN

PREP TIME:
10 minutes

COOK TIME:
30 minutes

SERVES
4

TOOLS

Cutting board

Knife

Large bowl

Kitchen towel

Parchment-lined baking sheet

Small saucepan

Spatula

4 large potatoes (russet preferred)

3 tablespoons canola oil

1 teaspoon salt

1 teaspoon black pepper

1 teaspoon garlic powder

2 tablespoons salted butter

2 tablespoons all-purpose flour

1 cup milk

8 ounces American cheese, in cubes or squares

¼ teaspoon chili powder

Fries are the classic side for burgers, chicken fingers, sandwiches, and even battered fish. They can also be seasoned in many different ways, depending on what flavor you're craving. These oven-baked "fries" are crispy, and since they're baked, they're healthier for you! Plus, the creamy sauce is perfect for dunking or drizzling on your fries.

1. **Preheat the oven and prepare the potatoes.**

Preheat the oven to 450°F. Wash the potatoes and leave the skin on. Set a potato on a cutting board so the long side is flat against the board. Grip the potato with your claw; then slice into it lengthwise to create planks. Lay each plank down flat and slice it into ½-inch sticks. Place each potato stick into a large bowl of water while you cut the rest of the potatoes. You can soak for up to 30 minutes, but you can move on to the next step once all the potatoes are cut.

2. **Rinse and dry off the potatoes.**

Drain the water into the sink and rinse the potato sticks. Using a kitchen towel, pat down and dry them very well.

ANOTHER IDEA: Have leftover chili? Perfect! Make chili cheese fries. Top your cooked fries with reheated chili, cheese sauce, sour cream, bacon bits, and green onions.

3. Season, toss, and bake the potatoes.

Place the potato sticks on a parchment-lined baking sheet, drizzle them with the oil, and add the salt, pepper, and garlic powder. Toss until evenly coated. Bake for 20 minutes; then gently toss again and bake for an additional 10 minutes.

4. Make the cheese sauce.

While the fries bake, melt the butter in a saucepan over medium heat. Add the flour and stir until smooth. Add in the milk, stir, and bring to a simmer. Add the cheese cubes and chili powder and stir steadily for 3 to 4 minutes or until thoroughly melted and smooth. Set aside. Once the fries are fully cooked, remove from the oven and serve with the cheese sauce.

STICKY HONEY BARBECUE WINGS WITH RANCH

NO NUTS

PREP TIME:
10 minutes

COOK TIME:
55 minutes

SERVES
4

TOOLS

2 large bowls

Whisk

Parchment-lined baking sheet

Tongs

Mixing spoon

1 cup all-purpose flour

1 teaspoon chili powder

1 teaspoon salt

1 teaspoon black pepper

1 teaspoon paprika

1 teaspoon garlic powder

1 teaspoon onion powder

20 chicken wings or drumettes

1 cup barbecue sauce

½ cup honey

Ranch dressing, for dipping

One of my favorite appetizers is a platter of saucy wings. The best part about wings is that you can toss them in any sauce once you know how to make them. These wings are sticky, juicy, and flavorful. You can enjoy them alone, have them as a side, or make them a meal by serving them with fries, celery, and carrots. Enjoy a restaurant favorite at home!

1. Preheat the oven and prepare the flour mixture.

Preheat the oven to 425°F. In a large bowl, whisk together the flour, chili powder, salt, pepper, paprika, garlic powder, and onion powder.

2. Coat and bake the wings.

Using your hands, take a wing and place it into the flour mixture. Toss until fully coated and place it on a parchment-lined baking sheet. Repeat this step for every wing and place them evenly in a single layer on the baking sheet. Bake for 45 minutes, using tongs to flip halfway through. Remove from the oven when wings are browned and crisp. Keep in mind that larger wings may take more time to cook.

HELPFUL HINT: Sometimes, as a cook, it may be tricky to know when food is safe to eat. Cooked chicken has an internal temperature of 165°F. If you're unsure, use a cooking thermometer to check. Another helpful sign to look out for is when the juices of the cut chicken run clear.

3. **Prepare the sauce and coat the wings.**

In a large bowl, mix together the barbecue sauce and honey until fully combined. Place the cooked wings in the sauce and toss until evenly coated.

4. **Caramelize and serve.**

Using tongs, place the coated wings back on the baking sheet in a single layer and bake for 8 to 10 minutes more until the barbecue sauce becomes caramelized (meaning the sugar in the sauce has become syrupy and sticky). Cool and serve with ranch dressing.

CRISPY CHICKEN TENDERS WITH SECRET SAUCE

NO NUTS

TOOLS

Parchment-lined baking sheet

Small bowl

Whisk

3 medium bowls

Tongs

Nonstick cooking spray

¼ cup honey

2 tablespoons yellow mustard

¼ cup barbecue sauce

½ cup mayonnaise

1¼ cups all-purpose flour

1¼ teaspoons seasoning salt

¼ teaspoon black pepper

¼ teaspoon paprika

2 large eggs

2 cups panko bread crumbs

16 boneless, skinless chicken tenderloins

Chicken tenders can be really fun to make and eat. They're juicy and crispy, and you can dunk them in this secret sauce—or go for barbecue, ranch, sweet-and-sour, or blue cheese sauce. Enjoy them alone or with a side of fries.

1. Preheat the oven.

Preheat the oven to 400°F.

2. Prepare the secret sauce.

In a small bowl, whisk together the honey, yellow mustard, barbecue sauce, and mayonnaise until combined. Set aside.

3. Prepare the flour, eggs, and panko mixes.

In a medium bowl, mix together the flour, salt, pepper, and paprika. In another medium bowl, whisk the eggs. Set both bowls aside. In a third medium bowl, put the panko bread crumbs.

DON'T HAVE IT? If you can't find chicken tenderloins in the meat section at your grocery store, use 2 pounds of chicken breast. Trim the fat and cut the chicken into 1-inch strips. If you don't have panko bread crumbs, you can use Italian bread crumbs instead.

4. **Bread the chicken tenders, bake, and serve.**

Working with one chicken tenderloin at a time, place the chicken in the flour mix and coat it, then dip it into the egg, and then coat it in the panko bread crumbs. Place the chicken on the lined baking sheet in a single layer. Repeat this step for each chicken tenderloin. Lightly spray the top of the tenders with cooking spray, bake for 18 to 20 minutes, and use tongs to turn the tenders when the cooking is halfway done. Depending on the size of your tenders, larger pieces may need more cooking time. Remove from the oven when the tenders are crisp and golden brown. Serve with a side of secret sauce.

SOUR CREAM AND CHIVE MASHED POTATOES

NO NUTS | VEGETARIAN

PREP TIME:
15 minutes

COOK TIME:
15 minutes

SERVES
6

TOOLS

Large pot

Ladle

Colander

Large bowl

Potato masher

Spatula

2½ pounds potatoes (Yukon Gold preferred), washed, peeled, and cubed

2 cups chicken broth, plus more as needed

2 tablespoons salt

½ cup heavy cream

½ cup sour cream

6 tablespoons salted butter, plus more for topping

⅛ teaspoon black pepper

¼ cup chopped chives

These fluffy, creamy, and tangy mashed potatoes pair well with almost any dish. I'm known for my mashed potatoes, and with this recipe, you will be, too.

1. Boil the potatoes.

Place the potatoes in a large pot. Add the broth, using more as needed to completely cover the potatoes. Bring to a boil over high heat; then lower the heat, put a lid on the pot, and simmer for 10 to 12 minutes, or until fork-tender. Wear oven mitts for the next steps, or ask an adult to help. After turning off the heat, move the pot to a cooler part of the stove. Reserve ¼ cup of the broth using a ladle, and drain the pot into a colander in the sink.

2. Mix and mash.

Place the potatoes, salt, heavy cream, sour cream, butter, and pepper in a large bowl. Use a potato masher to get them as smooth as you want. If they are too thick, add in the reserved broth.

3. Top the potatoes.

Using a spatula, scrape down the edges of the bowl and fluff the mashed potatoes. Top with the chives and more butter to taste.

CHOCOLATE-HAZELNUT SPREAD

PREP TIME:
15 minutes, plus 15 minutes to cool

MAKES
2½
CUPS

TOOLS

Blender

Tamper (optional)

Spatula or scraper

Mason jar (16-ounce) or container of your choice

½ cup peanut oil

3 cups roasted unsalted hazelnuts

½ teaspoon vanilla extract

1 cup milk chocolate chips

1 cup chopped dark chocolate

ANOTHER IDEA: Use unsalted roasted almonds to make chocolate almond butter.

If you love store-bought chocolate-hazelnut spread, you'll crave this homemade version even more. Spread it on bread, use it to top yogurt or fruit, or mix it into desserts.

1. Blend the hazelnuts.

Place the oil and hazelnuts in the blender. Secure the lid, but remove the fill cap. Start blending on low speed, and slowly increase to medium and then to high. Stop the blender and push the nuts down with a tamper (if using) or a spatula. Scrape the edges of the blender and add the vanilla. Continue to blend for about 1 minute, until the mixture is smooth.

2. Add the chocolate.

On medium speed, slowly add the chocolate chips and blend until thoroughly combined. Slowly add the dark chocolate and blend until combined. Increase the speed to high and blend for another 30 seconds.

3. Pour into the container.

Transfer the mixture into a mason jar. Blending on high makes the mixture warm, so let cool for 15 minutes before storing at room temperature or in the refrigerator for up to 2 weeks. If you keep it in the refrigerator, it will need to sit out for a bit to soften up before you can use it.

HOW TO MAKE SOUPS, SALADS, AND SANDWICHES

Chunky Chicken Noodle Soup PAGE 68

CHEF'S SALAD WITH RANCH DRESSING

PREP TIME:
10 minutes

SERVES
4

TOOLS

Large bowl
Rubber tongs

8 cups lettuce (Boston preferred), chopped

½ cup carrots, grated

¾ cup shredded cheddar cheese

¾ cup ham, cubed

½ cucumber (English preferred), sliced

8 cherry tomatoes, halved

⅓ cup bacon bits (optional)

4 hard-boiled eggs, sliced (page 37)

8 tablespoons ranch dressing

When it comes to salads, the toppings make all the difference. Great as a side or as a quick lunch, this classic salad is packed with cheddar, ham, eggs, and vegetables. You can always bulk this up with more veggies and leftover chicken.

1. **Assemble the main ingredients.**

Place the lettuce, carrots, cheese, ham, cucumber, tomatoes, and bacon bits (if using) in a bowl, and toss them together.

2. **Top and dress the salad.**

Top with the sliced eggs, drizzle with ranch dressing, and serve. Alternatively, you can make the salad look fancier: Use a large bowl or divide lettuce evenly among 4 individual bowls. You can use the lettuce as a bed and create vertical rows made up of each ingredient. Add a row of carrots, a row of cheddar cheese, a row of ham a row of cucumber, a row of tomatoes, a row of bacon (if using), and a row of eggs. Drizzle with dressing and serve.

ANOTHER IDEA: Instead of using a store-bought dressing, make your own! Use ½ cup mayonnaise, 1 tablespoon of vinegar, ½ tablespoon of sugar, ½ teaspoon of paprika, and salt and pepper to taste.

KALE CAESAR SALAD

NO HEAT NECESSARY | FAST | NO NUTS | VEGETARIAN

PREP TIME:
10 minutes

SERVES
4 TO **6**

TOOLS

Small bowl

Whisk

Cutting board

Paring knife

Large salad bowl

Tongs

½ cup plain **Greek yogurt**

4 tablespoons **lime juice**

1¼ tablespoon **extra-virgin olive oil, divided**

2 teaspoons **Worcestershire sauce**

1 teaspoon **Dijon mustard**

¼ teaspoon **salt, plus a pinch more**

⅛ teaspoon **black pepper**

½ tablespoon **garlic powder**

1¼ cups **grated Parmesan cheese, divided**

4 tablespoons **milk**

1 large bunch **kale, washed and dried**

1 cup **seasoned croutons**

Kale Caesar salad is easily one of my favorites. It's crunchy, creamy, cheesy, and tangy. You can use romaine lettuce instead of kale if you want a more traditional Caesar.

1. Make the dressing.

In a small bowl, whisk together the yogurt, lime juice, 1 tablespoon of olive oil, the Worcestershire sauce, mustard, ¼ teaspoon of salt, the pepper, garlic powder, and ½ cup of cheese. Whisk until combined. Add in the milk 1 tablespoon at a time until the dressing is your desired consistency.

2. Prep the kale and assemble the salad.

Lay a kale leaf on a cutting board. Using a paring knife, cut along the kale stem on both sides, and then remove the stem from the leaf. Repeat with the remaining leaves. Chop the kale into bite-size pieces and transfer to a large salad bowl. Add the remaining ¼ tablespoon of olive oil and a pinch of salt. Squeeze and knead the kale with your hands for 2 to 3 minutes, or until the leaves turn dark and silky. Add the croutons, dressing, and the remaining ¾ cup of cheese. Use tongs to toss until combined.

ANOTHER IDEA: Top your salad with some halved cherry tomatoes, cooked quinoa, or grilled chicken.

CLASSIC GRILLED CHEESE

PREP TIME:
5 minutes

COOK TIME:
25 minutes

SERVES
4

TOOLS

Butter knife

Nonstick skillet

Spatula

Cutting board

Bread knife

4 tablespoons unsalted butter, room temperature

8 slices sourdough or other sandwich bread

4 slices mozzarella cheese

4 slices sharp cheddar cheese

My family is full of grilled cheese lovers, and this version is one of our go-tos! Gooey cheese and buttery bread make this a win for a quick lunch or dinner. Pair it with Creamy Tomato Soup (page 67) and don't forget to dunk!

1. Butter the bread.

Generously butter one side of each piece of bread.

2. Assemble and grill the sandwiches.

Heat a nonstick skillet over medium heat. Place one slice of bread buttered-side down on the pan. Top with one slice of mozzarella cheese and one slice of cheddar cheese. Place another slice of bread on top, buttered-side up. Cook for 3 minutes or until golden brown, flip, and cook for another 3 minutes or until golden brown. Remove from the pan and set aside on a cutting board or plate. Repeat with the remaining bread and cheese; you should have 4 sandwiches. Slice the sandwiches in half and serve.

ANOTHER IDEA: To level up your grilled cheese, use two slices of salami or a couple of slices of fresh tomato.

BROCCOLI-CHEDDAR SOUP

NO NUTS

PREP TIME:
10 minutes

COOK TIME:
25 minutes

SERVES
4

TOOLS

Large pot

Wooden spoon

Whisk

Ladle

3 tablespoons unsalted butter

½ teaspoon garlic powder

½ medium white onion, chopped

3 tablespoons all-purpose flour

1 cup half-and-half

3 cups chicken broth

1 teaspoon salt, plus more as needed

⅛ teaspoon black pepper

4 cups broccoli florets

3 cups shredded cheddar cheese, plus more for topping

1 tablespoon chopped fresh parsley, for topping

This velvety soup brings together tender broccoli and creamy cheese, and is loaded with mouthwatering flavor. Pair it with your favorite sandwich or salad for a satisfying lunch.

1. Prepare the butter and cream mixture.

In a large pot, melt the butter over medium heat. Add the garlic powder and onion and sauté for 3 to 4 minutes, or until tender. Whisk in the flour and stir for 2 to 3 minutes, or until the flour is well incorporated, there are no lumps or white streaks, and the mixture has thickened. Slowly pour in the half-and-half and whisk for another minute, or until well blended.

2. Make the soup.

Add the broth and whisk until smooth. Make sure to mix well and whisk along the bottom to remove any lumps. Add the salt and pepper and bring to a boil. Add the broccoli and cook for 10 minutes, or until tender. Lower heat to a simmer, and use the wooden spoon to mix in the cheese until melted. Turn off the heat and season with salt to taste. Ladle into bowls and top with the extra cheese and parsley.

ANOTHER IDEA: For a touch more sweetness, add 1 cup of chopped carrots with the broccoli.

THE PERFECT BLT

PREP TIME:
10 minutes

COOK TIME:
20 minutes

SERVES
4

TOOLS

Baking sheet

Aluminum foil

Oven-safe cooling rack

Tongs

Paper-towel-lined plate

Butter knife

12 slices bacon

⅓ cup mayonnaise

8 slices rye bread, toasted

4 pieces green leaf lettuce, washed and dried

3 medium tomatoes, sliced in rounds

You know a sandwich is classic when it's known just by its initials. This recipe combines crunch, juiciness, and creaminess—all between slices of toasty bread.

1. Prepare the oven and baking sheet.

Preheat the oven to 400°F. Line a baking sheet with aluminum foil, and set an oven-safe cooling rack on top.

2. Cook the bacon.

Place the bacon strips on the cooling rack. Bake for 20 minutes, or until the bacon is crispy. Remove from the oven and use tongs to transfer the bacon to a plate lined with paper towels. Set aside.

3. Assemble the sandwiches and serve.

Spread mayonnaise on both halves of the bread. Layer the bottom of the bread with 1 piece of lettuce, 3 slices of bacon, and 3 to 4 slices of tomato. Add the top half of the bread to finish.

ANOTHER IDEA: Give these BLTs a garlicky kick by using a garlic aioli instead of plain mayo. In a small bowl, whisk together ⅓ cup of mayonnaise, ½ tablespoon of garlic powder, 1 tablespoon of lemon juice, 1 teaspoon of olive oil, ⅛ teaspoon each of salt and black pepper, and ½ teaspoon of Dijon mustard until blended.

BAGELWICH WITH ZESTY SAUCE

NO NUTS

PREP TIME:
10 minutes

COOK TIME:
15 minutes

SERVES
4

TOOLS

Medium skillet

Tongs

Paper-towel-lined plate

Baking sheet with rack

Small bowl

Whisk

Spoon

Cutting board

Knife

8 slices bacon

4 plain bagels, sliced in half

¼ cup extra-virgin olive oil

¼ cup lemon juice

1 tablespoon Dijon mustard

½ teaspoon salt

¼ teaspoon black pepper

4 slices provolone cheese

12 slices thin-sliced salami

12 slices thin-sliced mortadella

12 slices thin-sliced capicola

Sandwiches are a lunch (and even dinner) staple. It's no wonder because they're so versatile and filling. In this twist on a regular sandwich, a toasted bagel holds layer upon layer of tasty Italian meat and cheese with a zesty sauce. It hits the spot!

1. Preheat the oven and cook the bacon.

Preheat the oven to 375°F. Place the bacon in one layer on a cold skillet and cook over low heat for 8 to 12 minutes. In the middle of cooking, once the bacon starts to brown and release its fat, flip and fry until fully browned. Turn off the heat, move the pan to a cool part of the stove, and transfer the bacon to a plate lined with paper towels.

2. Toast the bagels.

While the bacon cooks, place the bagel halves facedown on the baking sheet rack and bake for 3 to 4 minutes. Remove from the oven and set aside.

3. **Make the zesty sauce.**

In a small bowl, whisk together the olive oil, lemon juice, Dijon mustard, salt, and pepper until emulsified. (*Emulsify* means smoothly combining two ingredients together that do not ordinarily mix easily.) Set aside. Keep in mind that you may have to rewhisk the sauce before using it.

4. **Assemble the bagelwiches.**

Place a slice of cheese on the face-up bottom half of the bagel. Layer 3 slices each of salami, mortadella, and capicola on top of the cheese. (Use fewer slices if the meat is not thinly cut.) Top with 2 pieces of bacon. Whisk the zesty sauce, and using a spoon, drizzle the sauce over the meat. Add the top part of the bagel. Cut in half and serve immediately. Repeat with the remaining bagels and fillings.

CHEESY TUNA MELT

NO NUTS

PREP TIME:
15 minutes

COOK TIME:
10 minutes

SERVES
4

TOOLS

Medium bowl

Whisk

Butter knife

Parchment-lined baking sheet

Spoon

Spatula

Bread knife

⅓ cup mayonnaise

⅛ teaspoon salt

⅛ teaspoon black pepper

1 teaspoon garlic powder

Juice of half a lemon

2 (6-ounce) cans tuna, drained

¼ cup finely chopped red onion

1 rib celery, finely chopped (optional)

½ teaspoon dried parsley

3 tablespoons unsalted butter, room temperature

8 slices sandwich bread

1 tomato, sliced in rounds

8 slices sharp cheddar cheese

Love tuna fish? I've got you covered. This tuna melt is crispy, creamy, and cheesy!

1. Preheat the oven and prepare the tuna mixture.

Preheat the oven to 400°F. In a medium bowl, whisk the mayonnaise, salt, pepper, garlic powder, and lemon juice until combined. Add the tuna, onion, celery (if using), and parsley. Mix until combined and set aside.

2. Assemble and bake sandwiches.

Butter one side of each slice of bread. Lay 4 slices butter-side down on the prepared baking sheet. Place about ½ cup of the tuna mixture, 2 tomato slices, and 2 slices of cheese on each slice of bread. Top each sandwich with another slice of bread, butter-side up. Bake for 8 to 10 minutes, or until golden brown. Remove from the oven and cut the sandwiches in half.

ANOTHER IDEA: Go "New York deli" style—use pumpernickel bread and add dill pickle slices.

CREAMY TOMATO SOUP

5 INGREDIENTS OR FEWER | NO NUTS

PREP TIME:
10 minutes

COOK TIME:
20 minutes

SERVES
4

TOOLS

Blender

Large pot

Wooden spoon

Ladle

2 (28-ounce) cans whole tomatoes

4 tablespoons salted butter

3 garlic cloves, finely minced

2 cups chicken broth

1 tablespoon salt, plus more as needed

½ teaspoon black pepper

½ cup heavy cream

Our family loves to dunk grilled cheese sandwiches into this soup or top it with homemade Parmesan-garlic croutons. To jazz it up, you can include some dried oregano and parsley when you add the salt and pepper. Or puree (smoothly blend) a can of drained whole roasted red peppers and add those along with the canned tomatoes.

1. Puree the tomatoes.

Pour the tomatoes and their juices into a blender. Blend until pureed.

2. Cook the soup.

In a large pot, melt the butter over medium heat. Add the garlic and sauté for 1 to 2 minutes, or until fragrant. Increase the heat to high; then add the pureed tomatoes, broth, salt, and pepper and bring to a rolling boil. Reduce the heat and simmer, uncovered, for 15 minutes. Stir in the heavy cream and add more salt to taste. Turn off the heat and ladle the soup into bowls.

HELPFUL HINT: To save on prep time, use canned crushed tomatoes instead of pureeing the whole tomatoes. The soup will be chunkier but still delicious.

CHUNKY CHICKEN NOODLE SOUP

NO NUTS

PREP TIME:
5 minutes

COOK TIME:
25 minutes

SERVES
6

TOOLS

2 large pots

Colander

Spatula

Mixing spoon

8 oz rotelle (wagon wheel) pasta

1 tablespoon extra-virgin olive oil

1½ cups carrots, chopped

1 cup yellow onion, chopped

½ teaspoon garlic powder

½ teaspoon salt, plus more as needed

¼ teaspoon black pepper

8 cups chicken broth

2 cups chicken thighs, finely chopped

Can it cure a cold? We don't know for sure, but with tender noodles, juicy chicken, and soft veggies, chicken noodle soup is definitely the ultimate comfort food that you can enjoy by the spoonful.

1. Cook the pasta.

Bring a large pot of well-salted water to a boil over high heat. Cook the rotelle for 9 to 12 minutes, or until al dente. (Al dente isn't just fun to say; it comes from the Italian term "at the tooth." This means your pasta has a pleasing texture—soft but with a bit of firmness and "bite" to the pasta noodles.) Drain and set aside.

2. Cook the vegetables.

Meanwhile, heat a large pot over medium heat. Add the olive oil, carrots, onion, garlic powder, salt, and pepper. Cook for 10 minutes, or until the vegetables are soft and tender.

3. Add the broth and noodles, and simmer.

Raise the heat to high, add the broth to the pot, and bring to a boil. Reduce the heat to medium-low and simmer for 10 minutes. Add the chicken and simmer for 3 to 4 minutes, or until chicken is cooked through. Taste the broth (letting it cool in a spoon so you don't burn your tongue) and, if you'd like it saltier, gradually adjust with salt to taste. (Remember that store-bought chicken broth often has a lot of salt already.) Add the cooked wagon wheel noodles, stir, and serve.

CHUNKY CREAM OF POTATO SOUP

NO NUTS

PREP TIME:
20 minutes

COOK TIME:
45 minutes

SERVES
6

TOOLS

Large pot

Tongs

Paper-towel-lined plate

Wooden spoon

Whisk

Potato masher

6 slices bacon, roughly chopped

4 tablespoons butter

1 medium yellow onion, chopped

2 garlic cloves, minced

⅓ cup all-purpose flour

5 medium Yukon Gold potatoes, peeled and cubed (¾-inch)

4 cups chicken broth

2 cups whole milk

½ cup sour cream

1½ teaspoons salt

1 teaspoon black pepper

Great for chilly or rainy days, potato soup is always cozy and comforting. It's creamy, full of flavor, and packed with lots of chunky bits of potato. This soup recipe is from my mother, Milagro, and I enjoyed it growing up. I hope it will become one of your favorites, too!

1. Fry the bacon.

In a large pot, cook the bacon pieces over low heat for 8 to 12 minutes. Flip often for even browning. Remove the bacon bits from the heat, transfer them to a plate lined with paper towels, and set aside. Leave the bacon grease in the pot.

2. Make a roux.

A roux (a French word pronounced "rue") is a mixture of fat and flour, and it is used to thicken sauces and soups. Switch to medium heat and add the butter and onion. Cook until the onion is translucent (see-through) for about 3 to 5 minutes. Add the garlic and cook until fragrant, for 30 seconds or so. Add the flour evenly across the ingredients and mix until smooth. You can use the spoon or a whisk to make the roux as smooth as possible.

3. Make the soup.

Add potatoes and chicken broth to the pot. Mix in the milk, sour cream, salt, and pepper. Mix all the ingredients until combined. Set to high heat and bring to a boil for about 10 minutes, or until the potatoes are tender. Reduce to medium-low to simmer, and use a potato masher to softly mash and break apart the potatoes. Be careful not to mash the potatoes entirely, but to create a smoother soup with smaller chunks. Simmer the soup for 30 minutes and serve. You can mix in the bacon pieces to the pot of soup, or you can top your bowls with bacon when serving.

CHAPTER 6

HOW TO
MAKE MAIN COURSES

Cheeseburgers with Secret Sauce PAGE 88

THIN-CRUST PEPPERONI PIZZA

NO NUTS

PREP TIME:
15 minutes

COOK TIME:
20 minutes

SERVES
4

TOOLS

Large mixing bowl

Wooden spoon

Rolling pin

12-inch nonstick pizza pan

2½ cups all-purpose flour, plus more for dusting counter

1 tablespoon baking powder

1 teaspoon salt

1 tablespoon extra-virgin olive oil

¾ cup water, plus more if needed

½ cup pizza sauce

1½ cups shredded mozzarella cheese

12 pepperoni slices

⅓ teaspoon dried oregano

¼ teaspoon red chili flakes (optional)

This homemade pie is cheesy, saucy, and topped with crispy pepperoni. Once you know how to make the dough, you can let your inner chef shine and add toppings of your choice.

1. **Preheat the oven and prepare the dough.**

Preheat the oven to 400°F. In a large mixing bowl, put the flour, baking powder, and salt. Mix until combined. Add the olive oil to the water; then pour it into the dry mixture bit by bit. Hold back some of the liquid, stir, and continue this process until the dough is not dry, adding more water if necessary. Once the dough is mixed, start kneading with your hands and form a ball.

2. **Assemble the pizza.**

Dust your counter or surface with flour; then place the dough on it and dust it lightly with flour. Use a rolling pin to roll the dough from the center to the edges. Turn it from time to time to ensure a round shape while you roll. You can use your hands to shape it as well. Place the dough onto the pizza pan and use your fingers to form a thin crust around the dough. Top with the pizza sauce, cheese, pepperoni, oregano, and chili flakes (if using). Bake for 15 to 17 minutes, or until golden brown, and serve.

BARBECUE-GLAZED MINI MEATLOAVES

NO NUTS

PREP TIME:
10 minutes

COOK TIME:
20 minutes

MAKES
12
MEAT-LOAVES

TOOLS

Medium bowl

Whisk

Large bowl

Mixing spoon

12-cup standard muffin tin

Spoon

⅓ cup ketchup

½ cup barbecue sauce, divided

1 tablespoon brown sugar

1 teaspoon Worcestershire sauce

1½ pounds extra lean ground beef

½ white onion, finely diced

⅛ teaspoon garlic powder

⅛ teaspoon dried parsley

1 teaspoon salt

½ teaspoon black pepper

¾ cup panko bread crumbs

1 egg

Meatloaf is one of my favorite comfort foods. These mini ones cook quickly and make great leftovers to pack for lunch. Serve with Sour Cream and Chive Mashed Potatoes (page 54).

1. Preheat the oven and prepare the glaze.

Preheat the oven to 425°F. In a medium bowl, whisk together the ketchup, ¼ cup of barbecue sauce, the brown sugar, and Worcestershire sauce until combined. Set aside.

2. Mix the meat mixture and bake.

In a large bowl, mix together the ground beef, onion, garlic powder, parsley, salt, pepper, bread crumbs, the remaining ¼ cup of barbecue sauce, and the egg until combined. Add ¼ cup of the glaze and mix well. Divide the mixture evenly among the muffin cups and top each meatloaf with 1 tablespoon of glaze. Bake for 20 minutes, or until cooked through. Remove from the oven, pop out the mini meatloaves (being careful not to touch any hot surfaces), and serve hot.

ANOTHER IDEA: To add sweetness, sauté the onions in a bit of olive oil for 2 to 3 minutes, until just tender, before adding them to the meat mixture.

VEGGIE RAMEN WITH "JAMMY" EGGS

NO NUTS

PREP TIME:
5 minutes

COOK TIME:
15 minutes

SERVES
2

TOOLS

Medium pot

Bowl with ice water

Colander

Large pot

Spoon

Tongs

Ladle

4 large eggs

2 packages dried ramen noodles, seasoning packets discarded

4 cups chicken broth

2 tablespoons white miso paste

2 large portabella mushrooms, sliced

2 cups baby spinach

1 cup fresh bean sprouts

½ cup chopped green onions

1 teaspoon sesame seeds

Sriracha (optional)

A savory broth with noodles, mushrooms, spinach, and "jammy" eggs—this is comfort food in a bowl.

1. Boil and cut the eggs.

Bring a medium pot of water to a boil over high heat. Once boiling, reduce to a simmer and add the eggs. Cook for 8 minutes; then transfer the eggs to a bowl of ice water. Peel and cut the eggs in half. The yolk should be firm but soft and jammy on the inside.

2. Make the ramen noodles.

Refill the medium pot with water and bring to a boil over high heat. Add the noodles and cook for about 3 minutes. Drain into a colander and rinse with cold water. Set aside.

3. Make the broth.

Pour the broth into a large pot and bring to a simmer over medium heat. Add the miso paste and stir until blended. Mix in the mushrooms and spinach and simmer for 3 to 4 minutes, or until tender. Remove from the heat.

4. Assemble and serve the ramen.

Using tongs, divide the noodles between two bowls. Ladle in the broth and top with the eggs, bean sprouts, green onions, and sesame seeds, dividing evenly. Drizzle with the sriracha (if using).

ANOTHER IDEA: Make it a little bit sweet by drizzling some hoisin sauce on top. Add more protein with some sliced pan-seared tofu.

SWEET AND SPICY PORK TACOS

NO NUTS

PREP TIME:
15 minutes

COOK TIME:
10 minutes

SERVES
4

TOOLS

Medium bowl

Mixing spoon

Small bowl

Whisk

Medium skillet

Spatula

Plate

Paper towel

Spoon

1 cup diced pineapple

½ cup finely chopped red onion

Juice of 1 lime

Salt

black pepper

¼ cup garlic powder

⅛ teaspoon cayenne pepper

¼ teaspoon dried parsley

4 tablespoons soy sauce

1 tablespoon brown sugar

These pork tacos are sweet, savory, and the perfect excuse to make pineapple salsa. You can top them with cotija cheese (similar to feta) and serve with lime wedges.

1. Prepare the salsa.

In a medium bowl, stir together the pineapple, onion, and lime juice. Season with salt and black pepper to taste. Set aside.

2. Make the sauce.

In a small bowl, whisk the garlic powder, cayenne, parsley, soy sauce, brown sugar, and water until combined; then set aside.

3. Fry the pork filling.

In a medium skillet, heat the oil over medium heat. Add the pork strips and cook for 3 minutes on each side, or until the pork is no longer pink. Pour the sauce into the pan and let the pork sit and caramelize in the sauce for 1 minute. Stir and turn the pork in the sauce for another 1 to 2 minutes. Turn off the heat and move the pan to a cool part of the stove.

2 tablespoons water

2 tablespoons canola oil

1 pound boneless pork loin, cut into thin strips

12 (4.5-inch) flour or corn tortillas

4. Warm the tortillas.

Stack 6 tortillas on a plate and cover with a damp paper towel. Microwave them on high for 30 seconds to warm. Repeat with the remaining tortillas.

5. Fill the tortillas.

Fill the warmed tortillas with the pork mixture. Top with the pineapple salsa and serve.

HELPFUL HINT: Save on prep time by using ground pork instead of pork loin. Cook the ground pork in the sauce for 3 to 5 minutes, or until cooked through.

ONE-POT CHEDDAR AND SAUSAGE RIGATONI

NO NUTS

PREP TIME:
5 minutes

COOK TIME:
20 minutes

SERVES
4

TOOLS

Cutting board

Paring knife

Large pot with a lid

Spatula

4 links Italian sausage

1 tablespoon canola oil

8 ounces rigatoni

2 cups chicken broth

1 (14.5-ounce) can diced fire-roasted tomatoes

½ teaspoon garlic powder

½ teaspoon chili powder

⅛ teaspoon paprika

1 teaspoon salt

½ teaspoon black pepper

1 cup cheddar cheese, shredded, plus more for topping

1 tablespoon fresh parsley, chopped

Boost your macaroni and cheese with this warm, hearty meal. My girls love this pasta, not only because of the cheese and sausage but also because it cooks up so quickly.

1. Brown the sausage.

With a paring knife, carefully cut the sausage casing lengthwise and remove the sausage. Discard the casing. In a large pot, heat the oil over medium heat. Crumble the sausage into the pot and cook for 5 minutes, or until fully cooked.

2. Add the pasta and cook.

Add the rigatoni, broth, tomatoes, garlic powder, chili powder, paprika, salt, pepper, and cheese to the pot. Stir together and bring to a boil over medium-high heat. Reduce the heat to low, cover, and cook, stirring frequently, for 15 minutes, or until the pasta is tender.

3. Serve.

Turn off the heat, move the pot to a cool part of the stove, and plate the pasta. Top with additional cheese and parsley.

HELPFUL HINT: To save time, use precooked turkey sausage. Just slice it up and panfry for a few minutes before continuing with the recipe.

STUFFED PASTA SHELLS

NO NUTS | VEGETARIAN

TOOLS

Large pot

Colander

Medium bowl

Mixing spoon

Square baking dish

Cutting board

Spoon

12 jumbo pasta shells

4 cups ricotta cheese

1 (10-ounce) package frozen spinach, thawed, excess water squeezed out

2 teaspoons garlic powder

2 teaspoons onion powder

½ teaspoon salt

1 teaspoon black pepper

2 eggs

1 cup canned tomato sauce, divided

1 cup shredded mozzarella cheese

¼ cup grated Parmesan cheese

2 tablespoons chopped fresh parsley

Shake up spaghetti night with these ricotta-stuffed shells. Serve with garlic bread or a side of Kale Caesar Salad (page 59).

1. Preheat the oven and boil the shells.

Preheat the oven to 350°F. Bring a large pot of well-salted water to a boil over high heat. Add the shells and cook for 12 to 15 minutes, or until soft but still firm in the center. Drain and set aside.

2. Make the cheese and spinach filling.

In a medium bowl, mix the ricotta cheese, spinach, garlic powder, onion powder, salt, pepper, and eggs until well combined.

3. Stuff and bake the shells.

Spread half the tomato sauce evenly on the bottom of a square baking dish. On a cutting board, spoon the cheese mixture into the shells; then place them in the baking dish. Spoon the rest of the tomato sauce on top of the shells and sprinkle with the mozzarella cheese. Bake for 10 minutes, or until the cheese melts. Remove from the oven and top with the Parmesan cheese and parsley.

SUPER CHEESY MAC AND CHEESE

NO NUTS | VEGETARIAN

PREP TIME:
15 minutes

COOK TIME:
50 minutes,
plus
10 minutes
to cool

SERVES
6

TOOLS

9-by-13-inch
baking pan

Small bowl

Mixing spoon

Large pot

Colander

Large
saucepan

Whisk

Spatula

Nonstick cooking spray

3 tablespoons unsalted
butter, divided

1 cup Italian-style
bread crumbs

2 cups Colby cheese

1 pound elbow macaroni

3 tablespoons all-
purpose flour

1 teaspoon salt

¼ teaspoon black pepper

3 cups whole milk

4 cups sharp cheddar cheese

Macaroni and cheese can be a main course or a side. It's also a great dish to know how to make for parties, holidays, and other big get-togethers.

1. Preheat the oven and grease the pan.

Preheat the oven to 400°F. Grease a 9-by-13-inch pan with nonstick cooking spray.

2. Make the bread crumb topping.

Melt 1 tablespoon of butter. In a small bowl, mix together the melted butter, bread crumbs, and Colby cheese until combined. Set aside.

3. Cook the pasta.

Bring a large pot of well-salted water to a boil over high heat. Cook the macaroni for 8 to 10 minutes, or until al dente. Drain into a colander, but reserve ½ cup of pasta water and set aside.

4. **Make the cheese sauce.**

In a large saucepan, melt the remaining 2 tablespoons of butter over medium-low heat. Add the flour, salt, and pepper, and whisk until smooth. Mix for 2 to 3 minutes continuously to make a roux. Slowly whisk in the milk and bring to a boil; then reduce the heat to a simmer. Add the reserved pasta water and cheddar cheese and whisk until combined. Using a spatula, stir the pasta into the cheese sauce until fully coated. Turn off the heat, carefully transfer the mixture to the greased pan, and sprinkle generously with the bread crumb topping. Bake for 30 minutes or until the top is golden brown and the mac and cheese is bubbling. Remove from the oven and let cool for 10 minutes before serving.

SPAGHETTI AND MEATBALLS

NO NUTS

PREP TIME:
15 minutes

COOK TIME:
40 minutes

SERVES
4

TOOLS

Large bowl

Nonstick baking sheet

Spatula

2 large pots with lids

Colander

Tongs

1 egg, beaten

2 cloves of garlic, chopped

¾ teaspoon salt

¼ teaspoon black pepper

1½ pounds ground beef

½ cup Italian bread crumbs

¼ cup Parmesan cheese, grated, plus more for topping

1 large (32-ounce) jar marinara sauce

½ pound spaghetti

When it comes to Italian food, one of the first recipes to put on your menu is spaghetti and meatballs. It's great for pasta nights! Tasty meatballs, al dente spaghetti, and Parmesan cheese—delizioso!

1. Preheat the oven.

Preheat the oven to 325°F and place the rack in the middle position.

2. Make the meatballs.

In a large bowl, put the egg, garlic, salt, pepper, beef, bread crumbs, and cheese. Using your hands, combine and knead the meat mixture together. Do not overwork it and stop as soon as it's combined. Roll the mixture into golf-ball-size meatballs and place them ½ inch apart on a large nonstick baking sheet.

3. Cook the meatballs.

Bake the meatballs for 10 minutes, use a spatula to flip them, and bake for another 10 minutes until browned and almost cooked through. Remove from the oven and set aside.

STORE IT: Cooked meatballs in sauce can be stored in an airtight container in the freezer for up to 3 months. (Let them cool before storing.) To reheat, thaw them in the refrigerator overnight; then transfer to a saucepan until the meatballs are warmed through, using lower heat. Too much stirring may break apart the meatballs, so be careful. Make some pasta, and you're good to go for another meal.

4. Prepare the marinara sauce.

In a large pot, bring the marinara to a simmer over medium heat. Transfer the meatballs to the marinara sauce, cover with a lid, and simmer for 10 minutes.

5. Cook the pasta.

While the sauce simmers, bring a large pot of well-salted water to a boil over high heat. Cook the spaghetti for 8 to 12 minutes, or until al dente. Use a colander to drain the spaghetti.

6. Assemble the spaghetti and meatballs.

Carefully transfer the spaghetti into the marinara sauce with the meatballs. Using tongs, toss the spaghetti until fully coated in sauce. Place the spaghetti and meatballs on plates, sprinkle with additional cheese, and serve.

STEAK FAJITAS

NO NUTS

PREP TIME:
20 minutes

COOK TIME:
25 minutes

SERVES
6

TOOLS

Large bowl

Whisk

Tongs

Baking sheet

¼ cup soy sauce

2 tablespoons lime juice

1½ tablespoons extra-virgin olive oil

1 teaspoon garlic powder

1 teaspoon chili powder

Salt

black pepper

2 pounds flank steak, thinly sliced

1 yellow bell pepper, sliced

1 red bell pepper, sliced

1 red onion, sliced

Corn tortillas, warmed, for serving

There's nothing like a family fajita night! Lay out your favorite fixings, like limes, salsa, diced avocado, shredded cheese, and sour cream, for build-your-own fajita fun.

1. Preheat the oven and marinate the steak.

Preheat the oven to 425°F. In a large bowl, whisk together the soy sauce, lime juice, oil, garlic powder, and chili powder. Season with salt and black pepper to taste. Using tongs, add the steak, bell peppers, and onion. Let the meat and veggies marinate for 5 minutes.

2. Cook the fajitas.

Pour the mixture onto a baking sheet and spread evenly. Bake for 15 minutes, tossing the mixture halfway through. Switch the oven to the broiler setting on high, and broil for 3 minutes to get it sizzling. Watch carefully to make sure it doesn't burn. Remove from the oven and serve with the warmed tortillas and your favorite fixings.

ANOTHER IDEA: Add creaminess with an avocado crema. In a blender, combine 1 pitted and peeled avocado, ½ cup of plain Greek yogurt, ¼ teaspoon of garlic powder, the juice of 1 lime, salt, and black pepper, blending until smooth.

CHEESEBURGERS WITH SECRET SAUCE

NO NUTS

PREP TIME:
10 minutes

COOK TIME:
25 minutes

SERVES
4

TOOLS

Small bowl

Whisk

Medium mixing bowl

Plate

Large skillet with lid

Spatula

Spoon

½ cup mayonnaise

2 tablespoons ketchup

1 tablespoon pickle relish

1 pound ground chuck beef

½ teaspoon salt

¼ teaspoon black pepper

4 slices cheddar cheese

4 burger buns, toasted

4 pieces green leaf lettuce, washed and dried

4 tomato slices

You don't have to fire up the grill to cook a cheeseburger! These are made on your stovetop. You can top them with your favorite fixings, like pickles, red onions, ketchup, mustard, and mayonnaise. Serve them with Crispy Oven-Baked Fries (page 48).

1. Make the secret sauce.

In a small bowl, whisk together mayonnaise, ketchup, and relish until combined. Set aside.

2. Prepare the burger patties.

In a medium bowl, place the ground beef, salt, and pepper, and mix to combine with your hands. Do not overwork. Divide the meat into 4 equal portions. Place one piece on a plate, and gently press to form a patty about 1 inch thick. Use your fingers to form an edge around the patty. You will end up with a small dimple or moat in the center. Repeat this process with each portion.

3. Cook the burgers.

Heat a large skillet over medium-high heat. Place the patties in the skillet, and cook for 9 minutes on each side. This will make medium-well burgers with a bit of pink inside. Burgers should be seared until browned halfway up the sides of the patties. Turn off the heat, move the pan to a cool part of the stove, and place a cheddar cheese slice on top of each burger. Cover the skillet with the lid for 2 to 3 minutes to let the steam melt the cheese.

4. Assemble the cheeseburgers.

Using a spoon, spread 1 or 2 tablespoons of secret sauce onto the top bun. Place 1 piece of lettuce on top of the sauce. Transfer the burger patty onto the bottom half of the bun. Top with 1 slice of tomato and any other favorite toppings of your choice, and complete by adding the top of the bun to the burger. Repeat with the remaining burgers and serve.

HOW TO MAKE DESSERTS

Confetti Vanilla Cupcakes PAGE 104

CANNOLI DIP

PREP TIME:
10 minutes

SERVES
8

TOOLS

Stand mixer or hand mixer

Large bowl

Spatula

Serving bowl

1 cup ricotta cheese

4 ounces (1 cup) cream cheese, room temperature

1 cup confectioners' sugar, plus more to taste

1 teaspoon vanilla extract

⅔ cup mini chocolate chips, plus more for topping

8 pizzelle cookies, broken into pieces

Did you know cannoli *means "little tubes" in Italian? These are Italian waffle pastries stuffed with a sweet cheese filling and sometimes dipped in chocolate. This easy version uses all the same ingredients and pizzelle cookies (classic Italian cookies that are made by being pressed between two iron plates like waffles) for dipping! If you can't find pizzelle, broken-up waffle or sugar cones will work, too!*

1. Mix the dip.

Using a stand mixer or in a large bowl with a hand mixer, combine the ricotta cheese, cream cheese, and confectioners' sugar on medium speed for 3 to 5 minutes, or until light and fluffy.

2. Add the vanilla and chocolate chips.

Add the vanilla and continue to mix for another 30 seconds. Taste the mixture, and if it isn't sweet enough, add more confectioners' sugar. Use a spatula to scrape down the sides of the bowl, and fold in the mini chocolate chips until well combined. Transfer to a serving bowl and top with additional chocolate chips. Serve with the pizzelle cookie pieces for dipping.

ANOTHER IDEA: To make the dip a little fancier, swap the cream cheese for mascarpone. Add more texture by adding chopped pistachios or more chocolate chips.

SUPER MOIST BANANA BREAD

NO NUTS | VEGETARIAN

PREP TIME:
20 minutes

COOK TIME:
1 hour, plus
1 hour to cool

SERVES
8 TO 10

TOOLS

9-by-5-inch
loaf pan

Parchment
paper

2 medium
bowls

Whisk

Spatula

Large bowl

Hand mixer

Wire cooling
rack

Nonstick cooking spray

1½ cups all-purpose flour

1 teaspoon baking powder

1 teaspoon baking soda

3 or 4 ripe bananas, mashed

½ cup sour cream

½ cup unsalted butter,
softened

1 cup granulated sugar

1 large egg

1 teaspoon vanilla extract

If you have overripe bananas, this is a great way to use them up. This is my mother's delicious banana bread recipe—it's moist inside with a perfectly crunchy crust!

1. Preheat the oven and prepare the pan.

Place the rack in the middle position and preheat the oven to 350°F. Grease a pan with cooking spray, line the pan with parchment paper, and set aside.

2. Mix the dry ingredients.

In a medium bowl, whisk together the flour, baking powder, and baking soda and set aside.

3. Prepare the wet ingredients.

In a medium bowl, combine the bananas and sour cream and set aside.

4. Make the banana bread batter and bake.

In a large bowl, use the hand mixer to cream the butter and sugar using medium speed. Add the egg and vanilla and beat until smooth. Slowly add in the dry ingredient mixture, using the mixer on low speed, until combined. Pour the batter into the loaf pan and bake for an hour, or until a toothpick inserted in the center comes out clean. Remove from the oven and cool for an hour before serving.

CHEWY OATMEAL COOKIES

NO NUTS | VEGETARIAN

PREP TIME:
15 minutes

COOK TIME:
10 minutes,
plus
5 minutes
to cool

MAKES
8 TO 10
COOKIES

TOOLS

Baking sheet

Parchment
paper or
silicone mat

Small bowl

Whisk

Medium bowl

Hand mixer

Spatula

Spoon

Wire cooling
rack

⅓ cup all-purpose flour

¼ teaspoon baking soda

⅛ teaspoon sea salt

⅓ teaspoon ground cinnamon

3 tablespoons unsalted butter, softened

3 tablespoons brown sugar

1 tablespoon granulated sugar

¼ teaspoon vanilla extract

1 egg yolk

½ cup old-fashioned rolled oats

These cookies are chewy and sweet with a hint of salt and just the right amount of oats. Get creative with different mix-ins, like peanut butter chips, chocolate chips, chopped walnuts, or raisins. These cookies pair perfectly with a tall glass of milk.

1. Prepare the oven and baking sheet.

Preheat the oven to 350°F. Line a baking sheet with parchment paper or a silicone mat and set aside.

2. Mix the dry ingredients.

In a small bowl, whisk together the flour, baking soda, salt, and cinnamon and set aside.

3. Prepare the batter.

In a medium bowl, beat the butter, brown sugar, and granulated sugar with a hand mixer until light and fluffy. Add the vanilla and egg yolk and mix until combined. Using a spatula, scrape down the sides of the bowl. Slowly fold in the dry ingredients and rolled oats until thoroughly combined.

4. Bake the cookies.

Spoon the batter onto the prepared baking sheet. You should have 8 to 10 cookies. Bake for 10 minutes, or until the cookies are golden brown with soft centers. Remove from the oven, cool for 5 minutes, and transfer to a cooling rack.

STORE IT: You can freeze oatmeal cookie dough to use later. Place the cookie dough into balls on a baking sheet and freeze for 1 to 2 hours. Once frozen, store in an airtight container for up to 1 month. When you're ready to bake, remove the dough from the freezer and let it come to room temperature before baking.

GREEN MINT CHOCOLATE MILKSHAKE

NO HEAT NECESSARY | NO NUTS | VEGETARIAN

PREP TIME:
15 minutes

SERVES
2

TOOLS

Blender

Medium bowl

Hand mixer

1 cup milk

1 frozen or fresh banana

8 drops green food coloring

1 cup ice (optional)

1 cup vanilla ice cream

1 teaspoon peppermint extract

½ cup chocolate chips

½ cup heavy cream, cold

1 tablespoon confectioners' sugar

¼ teaspoon vanilla extract

2 maraschino or fresh cherries, for topping

If you love peppermint and chocolate, this milkshake is for you! It's creamy and chocolaty, with just a hint of mint. Learning the base of this treat—ice cream, ice, and milk—opens up a world of milkshake possibilities!

1. Blend the milkshake.

In a blender on high speed, combine the milk, banana, food coloring, ice (if using), ice cream, peppermint, and chocolate chips. Blend until smooth and creamy.

2. Make the whipped cream.

In a medium bowl, using a hand mixer, whip together the heavy cream, confectioners' sugar, and vanilla for 3 to 4 minutes on medium-high speed, or until soft peaks form. The peaks should hold their shape.

3. Serve.

Pour the milkshakes into 2 tall glasses. Top them with the whipped cream, add a cherry, and serve immediately.

ANOTHER IDEA: Skip the peppermint extract and green food coloring, and instead add 6 chocolate sandwich cookies while blending for a cookies 'n' cream shake.

PERFECT CHOCOLATE CHIP COOKIES

PREP TIME:
10 minutes

COOK TIME:
15 minutes,
plus
5 minutes
to cool

SERVES
6

½ **cup butter, melted**

½ **cup granulated sugar**

½ **cup dark brown sugar**

1 **large egg, room temperature**

1 **teaspoon vanilla extract**

½ **teaspoon kosher salt**

½ **teaspoon baking soda**

1⅓ **cups all-purpose flour**

1 **cup large chocolate chips**

HELPFUL HINT: Chill the batter for 1 to 2 hours to cool off the butter in your batter and avoid flat cookies!

TOOLS

Large bowl

Spatula

Large cookie scoop or spoon

Parchment-lined baking sheet

Crispy on the edges and chewy in the middle, chocolate chip cookies are the best! Plus, these require no mixer or chilling. While the cookie dough might look like dessert, remember, this cookie dough isn't safe to eat.

1. Preheat the oven and prepare the cookie batter.

Preheat the oven to 350°F. In a large bowl, mix the butter, granulated sugar, and brown sugar. Add the egg and mix until combined. Add the vanilla and salt, and place the baking soda right into the vanilla and fold until thoroughly mixed. Add the flour and chocolate chips until fully combined (but don't overmix).

2. Shape and bake the cookies.

Using a cookie scoop or spoon, scoop out 6 balls of batter. (If using a spoon, the amount is about 3 tablespoons per cookies. Use your hands to roll the dough into balls.) Place them on the prepared baking sheet, about 2 inches apart. Clean up the edges by pressing them in. Bake for about 12 minutes, or until tops are lightly browned. Cool for 5 minutes and serve.

WHITE CHOCOLATE PEANUT BUTTER COOKIES

5 INGREDIENTS OR FEWER | VEGETARIAN

PREP TIME:
10 minutes

COOK TIME:
10 minutes, plus 10 minutes to cool

MAKES
12
COOKIES

1 cup smooth peanut butter

1 cup brown sugar, firmly packed

1 large egg

1 teaspoon baking soda

½ cup white chocolate chips

TOOLS

Parchment-lined baking sheet

Large bowl

Spatula

Small cookie scoop or spoon

Wire cooling rack

Peanut butter cookies should be chewy and nutty, and this version puts them over the top with white chocolate chips. The best part? They use only five ingredients and are ready in 30 minutes. Serve these with a tall glass of milk.

1. Preheat the oven.

Preheat the oven to 350°F.

2. Make the cookie batter.

In a large bowl, using a spatula, mix together the peanut butter, brown sugar, egg, and baking soda until well combined. Fold in the white chocolate chips.

3. Bake the cookies and enjoy.

Using a cookie scoop or spoon, scoop out 12 balls of batter. (If using the spoon, use your hands to roll the dough into balls.) Place the balls on the prepared baking sheet, about 2 inches apart. Bake for 9 to 10 minutes, or until the tops are lightly browned. Remove from the oven and let cool for 1 to 2 minutes before transferring to a wire rack to cool for another 5 minutes.

NO-BAKE
KEY LIME PIE

PREP TIME:
20 minutes,
plus
10 minutes
for chilling

SERVES
4

TOOLS

Medium bowl

2 spoons

Stand mixer or
hand mixer

Large bowl

Small bowl

4 (8-ounce)
mason jars

2 cups graham cracker crumbs

**3 tablespoons unsalted
butter, melted**

**1 (8-ounce) package of cream
cheese, softened**

**½ (14-ounce) can sweetened
condensed milk**

½ cup vanilla Greek yogurt

2 tablespoons key lime juice

**1 cup whipped cream,
for topping**

**2 tablespoons key lime zest,
for topping**

*Named after the Florida islands where
they grow, key limes have a sourer
flavor than regular limes do. They're
especially delicious when combined
in this traditional pie with condensed
milk, cream cheese, and yogurt. If you
can't find key limes, you can use regular
limes instead. Just be sure to zest your
limes before juicing!*

1. **Make the pie crust crumble.**

In a medium bowl, stir together the graham
cracker crumbs and butter until combined.
Set aside.

2. **Mix the key lime cream.**

Using a stand mixer or an electric hand mixer
and large bowl, beat together the cream
cheese, condensed milk, yogurt, and key lime
juice on medium speed for 5 minutes, or until
the mixture is smooth. Place the bowl in the
refrigerator to chill for 10 minutes.

3. Layer, add toppings, and enjoy.

Transfer 4 tablespoons of the pie crust crumble to a small bowl and set aside. Using a spoon, evenly divide the remaining crumble among the jars. With clean hands, press down on the crumble to pack it tightly into the bottom of the jar. Evenly divide the key lime cream filling among the jars. Top each jar with a dollop of whipped cream, 1 tablespoon of crumble, and ½ tablespoon of key lime zest. Serve immediately.

ANOTHER IDEA: If you're feeling fancy, top your jars with slices of key lime, a vanilla wafer for some crunch, or fresh berries.

CHOCOLATE GLAZED DONUTS

VEGETARIAN

PREP TIME:
15 minutes

COOK TIME:
10 minutes,
plus
30 minutes
to cool

SERVES
12

TOOLS

12-cup nonstick
donut pan

Large bowl

Spatula

Piping bag or
spoon

Small bowl

Small spatula

Wire cooling
rack

Nonstick cooking spray

2 cups all-purpose flour

⅔ cup granulated sugar

2 teaspoons baking powder

½ teaspoon nutmeg

½ teaspoon salt

¾ cup buttermilk

2½ tablespoons butter, melted

2 large eggs, beaten

1 teaspoon vanilla extract

1 cup chocolate chips

1 teaspoon coconut oil

Sprinkles, for topping

Covered with chocolate and topped with sprinkles, these donuts are yummy for dessert or an occasional breakfast treat. Donuts are usually deep-fried, but this version is baked for a healthier version that's just as good.

1. Preheat the oven and grease the pan.

Preheat the oven to 425°F and grease a donut pan with nonstick cooking spray.

2. Make the donut batter.

In a large bowl, put the flour, sugar, baking powder, nutmeg, and salt, and mix until combined. Mix in the buttermilk, butter, eggs, and vanilla. Stir until combined, but be careful not to overmix the batter, which can result in tough or dense donuts.

3. Pour and bake the donuts.

Transfer the batter into a piping bag (with the tip cut off) and carefully pour the batter into the donut pan evenly. If you don't have a piping bag, spoon the batter into the pan as evenly as possible. Bake for 9 to 10 minutes or until golden brown. Cool for 10 minutes.

4. Make the chocolate glaze.

In a small bowl, combine the chocolate chips and coconut oil. To melt the chocolate, microwave at 50 percent power for 1 minute. Remove, stir with a spatula, and continue heating in 15-second intervals until completely melted.

5. Dip, sprinkle, and serve.

Once your donuts have cooled, flip the donuts and place them on a cooling rack. Use the bottom of the donut as the new top. It will be smoother than the opposite side. Dip the top side of each donut in the chocolate glaze, place on the rack, and add sprinkles. Repeat this step for each donut, and allow the glaze to set for 20 minutes or until it's hardened before serving.

CONFETTI VANILLA CUPCAKES

NO NUTS | VEGETARIAN

PREP TIME:
10 minutes

COOK TIME:
20 minutes,
plus
30 minutes
to cool

SERVES
24

TOOLS

2 (12-cup)
muffin tins

24 paper liners

Large bowl

Whisk

Hand mixer

Spatula

Wire cooling
rack

Frosting
spatula or
piping bag

3 cups all-purpose flour

1¾ cups granulated sugar

1½ teaspoon baking powder

¾ teaspoon salt

4 large eggs

¾ cup canola oil

1 cup milk

1 tablespoon vanilla extract

½ cup rainbow sprinkles, plus
more for topping

2 cups vanilla frosting

Confetti cupcakes are so much fun to eat, and these have the colorful sprinkles in the cake to prove it! They're also a great dessert to share at your next bake sale, birthday party, or potluck. These are soft and moist and can be made in one bowl!

1. Preheat the oven and prepare the tins.

Place the rack in the middle position and preheat the oven to 350°F. Line the muffin tins with paper liners and set aside.

2. Mix the dry ingredients.

In a large bowl, whisk together the flour, sugar, baking powder, and salt until combined.

3. Add the wet ingredients.

Add the eggs, oil, milk, and vanilla. Using a hand mixer on medium speed, beat for about 3 minutes or until smooth. Fold in the sprinkles, but be careful not to overmix the sprinkles. Overmixing or waiting too long to pour the mixture into the pan can cause the color of the sprinkles to bleed into the batter, causing streaks in your cupcakes.

4. Fill the liners and bake.

Fill the cupcake liners about three-quarters full, and bake for 15 to 18 minutes or until golden brown. You can check if the cupcakes are done by inserting a toothpick in the center of one of them; if they are done, it will come out clean. Allow the cupcakes to cool in the pan for 5 minutes. Then transfer them to the cooling rack for another 25 minutes.

5. Decorate and serve.

Once the cupcakes are fully cooled, it's time to frost. Use the piping bag or frosting spatula to top the cupcakes evenly with frosting. Top with sprinkles! Repeat this step for the rest of the cupcakes and serve.

COOKIE CRUNCH BROWNIES

PREP TIME:
10 minutes

COOK TIME:
20 minutes

MAKES
16
BROWNIES

TOOLS

8-by-8-inch baking dish

Aluminum foil

Large bowl

Whisk

Spatula

Cutting board

Knife

Wire cooling rack

Nonstick cooking spray

12 tablespoons (1½ sticks) unsalted butter, melted

1½ cup granulated sugar

3 large eggs

¾ cup cocoa powder

½ teaspoon salt

2 teaspoons vanilla extract

1 cup all-purpose flour

20 chocolate sandwich cookies, divided

¼ cup milk chocolate chips

Can't decide if you want cookies or brownies? These brownies are fudgy and chewy with a crunch in the middle—the best of both worlds.

1. Prepare the oven and baking dish.

Preheat the oven to 350°F. Line an 8-by-8-inch baking dish with aluminum foil, grease with cooking spray, and set aside.

2. Make the brownie batter.

In a large bowl, whisk together the butter and sugar until well combined. Add the eggs one at a time and whisk until combined. Add the cocoa powder, salt, and vanilla. Use a spatula to mix well. Gently fold in the flour, and mix until the flour is just combined and no white streaks are visible.

3. Assemble the brownies and bake.

Pour half the brownie batter into the prepared baking dish and spread it evenly. Place 16 chocolate sandwich cookies on top of the batter. Pour the rest of the batter on top. Chop or crush the 4 remaining cookies and sprinkle on top of the batter. Sprinkle the chocolate chips on top. Bake for 20 minutes, or until a toothpick inserted in the center comes out clean. Remove from the oven and let cool on a wire rack. Cut into 16 squares.

ANOTHER IDEA: Make a white chocolate topping. Microwave 1/3 cup of white chocolate chips in a bowl for 1 to 1½ minutes on 50 percent power. Continue in 10-second intervals until fully melted. Stir until smooth and drizzle white chocolate over the brownies before slicing.

Chocolate Glazed Donuts PAGE 102

Measurement Conversions

VOLUME EQUIVALENTS	U.S. STANDARD	U.S. STANDARD (OUNCES)	METRIC (APPROXIMATE)
LIQUID	2 tablespoons	1 fl. oz.	30 mL
	¼ cup	2 fl. oz.	60 mL
	½ cup	4 fl. oz.	120 mL
	1 cup	8 fl. oz.	240 mL
	1½ cups	12 fl. oz.	355 mL
	2 cups or 1 pint	16 fl. oz.	475 mL
	4 cups or 1 quart	32 fl. oz.	1 L
	1 gallon	128 fl. oz.	4 L
DRY	⅛ teaspoon		0.5 mL
	¼ teaspoon		1 mL
	½ teaspoon		2 mL
	¾ teaspoon		4 mL
	1 teaspoon		5 mL
	1 tablespoon		15 mL
	¼ cup		59 mL
	⅓ cup		79 mL
	½ cup		118 mL
	⅔ cup		156 mL
	¾ cup		177 mL
	1 cup		235 mL
	2 cups or 1 pint		475 mL
	3 cups		700 mL
	4 cups or 1 quart		1 L
	½ gallon		2 L
	1 gallon		4 L

OVEN TEMPERATURES

FAHRENHEIT	CELSIUS (APPROXIMATE)
250°F	120°C
300°F	150°C
325°F	165°C
350°F	180°C
375°F	190°C
400°F	200°C
425°F	220°C
450°F	230°C

WEIGHT EQUIVALENTS

U.S. STANDARD	METRIC (APPROXIMATE)
½ ounce	15 g
1 ounce	30 g
2 ounces	60 g
4 ounces	115 g
8 ounces	225 g
12 ounces	340 g
16 ounces or 1 pound	455 g

Index

ACKNOWLEDGMENTS

To Gabby and Michaela, it fills my heart with happiness that you share the love of good food with your dad and me. We've been able to experience so much through travel, food, and culture together. I hope we can continue to make fun and delicious memories at home and abroad.

To Darasak, my partner in life and the kitchen. Thank you for always encouraging me to never give up and for giving me strength when I need it most.

To my mom, Milagro, and my dad, Francisco, thank you for teaching me the value of hard work and perseverance and for your sacrifice to give us a better life. I can never pay you back, but I appreciate it infinitely. Mom, your delicious recipes made me the cook I am today.

To Susana, thank you for being my best friend and supporting me through thick and thin. To Frank, thank you for your constant and never-failing encouragement. Your honesty and support help me become better.

I love you all.

To you, the reader, I hope you found something in this book that you can always take with you. Keep going—you can cook!

ABOUT THE AUTHOR

Nancy Polanco is a journalist and the creator of the popular online lifestyle site Whispered Inspirations (WhisperedInspirations.com). She shares simple, delicious recipes that bring people together, the best travel destinations for families to explore, and helpful tips to make life easier. She hopes to inspire readers to learn, try something new, and step out of their comfort zone. Nancy's work can be found in various print and online outlets like Universal Studios, the *Huffington Post,* and TODAY Parents. Follow her on Facebook (Whispered Inspirations) and Instagram, Twitter, and Pinterest under @whispersinspire for recipes and more.

CPSIA information can be obtained
at www.ICGtesting.com
Printed in the USA
JSHW011549030921
18386JS00004B/6

9 781648 763229